OFFICE HOURS

OFFICE HOURS

One Academic Life

H. N. Hirsch

QUID PRO BOOKS

New Orleans, Louisiana

Published in 2016 by Quid Pro Books.

ISBN 978-1-61027-333-6 (pbk)
ISBN 978-1-61027-338-1 (cloth)
ISBN 978-1-61027-337-4 (ebk)

QUID PRO BOOKS
Quid Pro, LLC
5860 Citrus Blvd., suite D-101
New Orleans, Louisiana 70123
www.quidprobooks.com

qp

Publisher's Cataloging-in-Publication

Hirsch, H. N. (Harry Nathan), 1952–
    Office hours : one academic life / H. N. Hirsch.
        p. cm. — (Journeys & memoirs)
    Includes bibliographical references.
    ISBN 978-1-61027-333-6 (paperback)

    1. Hirsch, H. N., 1952–. 2. College teachers—Ohio (U.S.)—Biography. 3. University of California (System)—History. I. Title. II. Series.

PS3551.D32 H16 2016   813'.34.5—dc22

Front cover image adapted from painting "Professor William D. Marks" (1886), by Thomas Eakins. Author photograph on back cover inset provided courtesy of Oberlin College.

CONTENTS

Prologue: June 1

1 • Politics 101 5

2 • Psych 101 11

3 • Geography 101 21

4 • Politics 201 25

5 • The Ivy League for Beginners 49

6 • The Ivy League: Advanced 69

7 • Accounting 103

8 • Drama: Advanced Seminar 149

9 • Gay Studies 177

10 • Psych 201 193

11 • Sociology 300: Imagining the Future 195

Epilogue: September 201

References 205

Acknowledgments 209

To John Burke, Nancy Rosenblum,
Ethel Klein, Jack Yeager,
and the memory of Tim Cook

I should not talk so much about myself if there were anybody else whom I knew as well.

— Henry David Thoreau

OFFICE HOURS

Prologue: June

Finally, summer. Another school year has ended, as it always does, with perfect weather. It is always hot for graduation, a natural law, the faculty sweating in dark robes meant for drafty medieval buildings. Then the students and parents leave and the weather turns lovely. Cool breeze, windows open. Everything in bloom.

I exhale. I cook. I sleep late. I think it's time to get another dog. I read a bit for pleasure, not for work. Students write me email notes thanking me for a course. One or two complain about their grade. Seniors say goodbye, some in lovely handwritten notes. I write my 7,396th letter of recommendation for law school.

Summer. Free time.

Time to watch movies. Old ones with strong women (I am, after all, a gay man) and new movies, the ones not about disasters or vampires. Movies have always been there for me when I want to relax or escape, even as a young child, home alone, both parents working, nothing to do after school until they came home except watch Chicago's *Early Show* on our old black and white TV. Then as an adolescent, needing escape as my family disintegrated, more movies, vibrant women, wit and bravado, a Katharine Hepburn festival courtesy of WGN, Chicago's hometown station. Even at twelve, I wanted to be Kate, not Spencer Tracy.

We needed wit and bravado back then, before Stonewall, before gay marriage. We needed wit and bravado and we needed to be tough, Susan Hayward tough, Susan Hayward-facing-the-gas-chamber tough (in *I Want to Live*, a film I would, decades later, show to my students studying the death penalty). I wanted to be Hepburn and Hayward and

1

I wanted to be Barbara Stanwyck in *The Lady Eve*. Who could possibly have wanted to be clueless Henry Fonda in that movie, defenseless putty in her extortionate hands?

As I got older, I wondered: What would my own movie look like? Would I be Vivien Leigh during the Civil War, tough, determined, never defeated, grasping, always grasping, for success, or would I be Vivien in *Streetcar*, a failure, pathetic, off to the nut house with her? I wondered.

I wonder still. Which am I?

How can one know? Who writes the script?

Who indeed.

I am in my sixties now, a shock. In my head I am thirty-five. Sixty came exactly a year after another shock, heart surgery—a surprise, not only to me but to the doctors, who have watched me closely, family history, terrible genes. If our parents were still alive I would sue them, I tell my sister. The purest luck, an alert internist, a mild pain at the base of the neck, I almost didn't go in. The heart is fine now, mended, they tell me.

Does a heart mend?

Time to ask.

Time to look. Time to look closely.

But where does one look, how does one see?

Which tale shapes the story? The young boy who loved books and movies and then, a bit later, the simple act of writing, anything, random words in pen or pencil, whose most cherished possessions were notebooks and folders containing schoolwork? The more-than-ordinarily awkward adolescent? The intellectual prodigy? The years at state universities, or the time in the Ivy League? The small colleges? The semivoluntary renunciation of academic status, perhaps?

What have I been and who am I now? Saint or prig? Historian or harridan? Critic or crybaby? What do I know and what do I seek? Wisdom or revenge? Closure or clarification?

Where is the heart of the story?

The early ambition? The self-doubt? The fears or the certainties? Demons or mentors? Teachers or students? Friends or enemies? Achievements or blunders? Books written or projects imagined but never begun?

Is the key a pithy quote, perhaps?

An obscure American radical, discovered in a course taught for the first time only in the last few years:

The most powerful narcotic in the world is the promise of belonging.

Ah yes. I see, the movie's twin themes. Belonging and success. Seeking, finding, losing, changing.

Rewriting the script. Look there for the story.

1

POLITICS 101

I remember when my life took shape, when it became inevitable that I would study politics: three moments over five months in the spring and summer of my seventeenth year.

Much later I will think: what if I hadn't turned sixteen in April, 1968? What if I had been a bit younger, or a bit older? Would I be a lawyer now? A psychologist? A professor of English? A drunk? Would I have taken shelter from the storm and made as much money as possible, stayed in the suburbs, as my older brother did? Or would it not have made any difference? What if I had turned twelve in 1968, or twenty?

Ah, but I did not. I turned sixteen the year everything in America changed forever.

April 5, just before my birthday. I turn on the radio while eating my morning cereal, as usual, and I hear that Martin Luther King Jr. has been assassinated. I stop eating and switch on the television. I tell my mother what has happened, yell to her through the bathroom door as she's getting ready for work. She comes out of the bathroom looking stricken.

I catch the school bus feeling like I'm in some sort of altered state, which I do not like or understand . . . do not like at all. My first thought: why am I so upset, this has nothing to do with me. But I sense that's not right, that something has happened, not just in the world but to me, and I feel an uncomfortable lurch beyond what I know. I am only dimly aware of Dr. King, but am aware of civil rights, of the tensions between white and black, so obvious in my home city of Chicago, even though

5

our suburb is all white. Eeny meany miney mo, catch a tiger by the toe. . . . I was thirty, a professor, before I learned that there were those in America who said "catch a nigger by the toe," not "tiger." In 1968 I didn't know anyone who didn't say "tiger," and I had only heard the N-word in one old movie.

I arrive at school. First period, math, a relief, geometry, lines and planes.

Second period, honors social studies. The teacher, Mrs. Smith, is the first African American teacher in my suburban high school, a school with no African American students in 1968 . . . no students of color at all. Mrs. Smith comes in, sits down. She is wearing a yellow and orange suit, high heels; she is perfectly made up, as always, a tall, striking woman. I was excited in September when I walked into her classroom and saw that I would be in a class with the first African American teacher in the school, and I liked her, liked her a lot. She had a wry sense of humor and she seemed to like me back.

This April day Mrs. Smith sits down but she does not speak. She tries to speak but she cannot. There is perfect silence in the class; even the usual class clown is silent. We all notice the silence, and we look around at each other, uneasy. We have never heard such silence in a classroom, not even during a test. It is as if no one is breathing or moving. I look over at my friend Ira, our eyes meet briefly, then we look again at Mrs. Smith. Some look down at their desks.

Mrs. Smith does not speak. She puts her hands on her desk. Time passes but Mrs. Smith does not speak.

Someone is supposed to be giving a report, so, after a while, he just starts speaking. Everyone turns to him, listens, then we begin discussing, as we would if Mrs. Smith were leading the class. We ask each other questions. I say something, then call on someone who seems to want to respond. Mrs. Smith sits, watches, listens perhaps. She looks as if she could cry at any moment. She sits with her hands on the desk.

We discuss the Tudors. We keep the discussion going for the full forty-five minutes. By the end of the class period the grief on her face is now combined with something else, a bit of gratitude, perhaps, that we let her just sit there and be.

The bell rings, we leave, quietly, reverently. In the hall someone says that Mrs. Smith doesn't have a class first period, so this was her first class of the day.

I assume I went through the rest of the school day as usual, although I cannot remember anything after second period. The look on Mrs. Smith's face, her inability to speak, sear into my brain. Nothing like this has ever happened to me, to us. There was the JFK assassination but we were eleven, too young to really grasp the magnitude of what had happened or what it could mean.

The next day Mrs. Smith is her usual self. In a group of sixteen-year-olds who gossip about everything and everyone, every teacher's foibles dissected constantly, no one ever mentions the class in which Mrs. Smith did not speak.

Two months later, the same second period social studies class. Early June, lovely weather in Chicago, lilacs blooming, a Wednesday morning. The night before Robert Kennedy was shot after winning the California primary.

My friend Ira has been an RFK enthusiast. I support McCarthy, along with our mutual friend Sharon, if "support" is an accurate description of what high school students do in suburban Chicago in a presidential campaign in 1968. Sharon and I went to a few meetings in downtown Chicago, where we were the only students not in college and felt completely out of place. We then do a bit of door-to-door canvassing in nearby suburbs. Ira does the same for RFK, and one day at a training session he meets young Ted, he tells us excitedly. Sharon and I support McCarthy because he seems more firmly opposed to the war, or he opposed it sooner than RFK. We did not understand the war in Vietnam, but we knew something was wrong. Even Walter Cronkite knew something was wrong. He told America so at the end of February.

Second period, social studies again, a few weeks before the end of the school year. The look on Ira's face perfectly matches the look on Mrs. Smith's face two months prior, and the similarity does something to my stomach. I try to comfort him before class starts, he is near tears, but I cannot think of what to say. What is the appropriate remark to a friend after a political assassination? They haven't taught us that yet in honors social studies.

Later that evening I call my friend, ask if he is ok, and he will mumble something, get off the phone quickly. I feel awful, dreadful, when I get off the phone, and I do not know what to do. I go out into the back yard and try to brush off the day, but the perfect spring weather feels jarring, out of place.

I do not understand what is happening in America, the neat and orderly and good America in which I grew up, the fifties America, when we moved to the suburbs and parents in our neighborhood let their children walk to school without worrying about their safety. The clean America, where everything worked out for the best and everyone went to college and got married and the girls did not get pregnant in high school, at least not in our school.

A few months later, after the Democratic convention in my hometown of Chicago, after the demonstrators are attacked by the police, after blood flows in the streets and parks I know so well, after my large and extended family divides into pro-Mayor Daley and anti-Mayor Daley factions—the same Mayor Daley for whom my Aunt Sylvia once worked—after that third earthquake, in just a few short months, I will begin to see. I will begin to see dimly.

I will begin to see or feel or sense that there is an official story, the story with which I grew up, was taught in school, the story I read every day in the *Chicago Daily News*, and then there is something else entirely: the real story.

I will begin to want the real story.

When they talk about it at all, our teachers and parents in 1968 and 1969 and 1970 will not tell us the real story, they do not know what it is. They grope. They struggle to shove what is happening into the familiar frame of that which is true and good, but their explanations fall flat, and we will see, some of us will see, or feel, or sense, that the frame cannot contain the picture, that this movie does not have a happy ending.

So at the age of sixteen, when the frame no longer fits, when the movie spins out of control, my life will acquire some shape, although I could not have told this to you if we had sat down and talked about it at the time. I could only have told you that some famous people who gave good speeches seemed to be getting shot for no apparent reason, that soldiers were dying in a far off place, and that no one could explain why they had to die, even when I started to ask.

It made people angry when I started to ask. It made them angry when I suggested an editorial in the high school newspaper about the war and the draft.

I could have told you if we had talked when I was sixteen that a political party to which my family had pledged undying loyalty was being pulled apart at the seams. I could have told you about the look on the face of a teacher I admired and a friend I loved in the spring of 1968, I could have told you about the day we taught our own class in second period social studies.

I could have told you about a college jock who lived nearby, who organized touch football games in the street when he was home—just like the Kennedys, he said, laughing—I could have told you how he came home bleeding and coughing one muggy summer night a few months after the two assassinations. Tear gas, he said, in Grant Park. My stomach lurched again. Grant Park.

Grant Park was the same park my grandmother would take me to after she visited our doctor on Jackson Street, the same park where my grade school class had eaten box lunches after visiting the Art Institute on a field trip.

Later, much later, in November 2008, I will think of the tear gas on the night Barack Obama won the presidency and spoke in Grant Park in front of a huge adoring crowd, the night I received an email with his name on it between the moment he was declared the winner and the moment he spoke in Grant Park, an email thanking me for my support, because I had given him money over and over again, like so many others who were 16 or 17 or 18 in 1968. "I have to get to Grant Park," the email said.

And I will think that in 1968 Obama was only seven years old. And on that night he won the election with 53 percent of the vote, when I cried because I was happy and proud, because I received an email message that some smart political operative decided to send out to still-gullible people like me, I wondered if he would have become president if he had been sixteen instead of seven in 1968. Would he have been able to stand it, I wondered, Dr. King's assassination and the riots that followed, the travesty of so many black soldiers in Vietnam coming home in a box or returning to broken limbs or nerves shattered by Agent Orange? Would he still have gone to the Harvard Law School, married someone like Michelle, traversed the line between the establishment and disgust, the disgust he heard at Reverend Wright's church on the South side, a church very close to a dry goods store once owned by my great-grandparents, would he have been able to walk that line with so much finesse and grace if he had been sixteen instead of seven in 1968? Might he, like someone else from my neighborhood, have dropped out of college and then fled to Canada to avoid the draft, and become a carpenter after his stint in rehab?

I thought about all that on the night Obama spoke in Grant Park, I thought about Ira and the tear gas, I thought about being sixteen in 1968. I didn't go to my friends Eve and Sandy's election night party, I wanted to be alone because I knew I would cry. I knew I would want to remember the moment, the moment before the inevitable mistakes and disappointments, compromises and disasters of a presidency. I knew I would again be the sixteen-year-old boy who had honors social studies, second period, with Mrs. Smith.

2
PSYCH 101

There was no place for me.

When I think of my childhood, my earliest years, when I think of growing up, that's what I think.

No place in the life of my family, which disappeared in slow motion, nor in the life of my country, which back then enforced a sexual morality as rigid as any Soviet gulag.

There was no place for me.

And:

I had to get away.

That is what I remember:

I had to get away.

Away from my family, from the Midwest, from middle-class suburbia.

If there is no place for me, I will find it somewhere else.

I was in a hurry.

Yes, I will find it somewhere else.

* * *

1952. The American Psychiatric Association, for the first time, publishes a list of mental disorders. This is, after all, America; we are an orderly people. God may be dying but Freud is alive and well, and he picked up considerable steam crossing the Atlantic.

In their list, the Association unequivocally defines "homosexuality" as an illness.

1952. Led by a man named Harry Hay—a name so similar to mine, I will think, decades later—a small group of these "diseased" homosexuals have begun meeting in Los Angeles. Communists, many of them, or fellow-travelers—Marx vies with Freud for popularity and allegiance among American intellectuals during and after World War II.

These men in Los Angeles meet in secret. Some of them think they can be arrested just for talking about their sexuality. They adopt a strange name, the Mattachine Society—named for an obscure medieval sect that was fond of masks—and never amount to very much, at least in terms of numbers. Within a few years the communists are gone and conservatives have taken over the organization.

1952. I am born on Easter Sunday, also Passover, in Chicago, to an observant Jewish family, still living in a large, extended immigrant clump, in an apartment building owned by my grandmother in a dicey neighborhood, Uptown (now completely gentrified). That week in April, "Wheel of Fortune" by Kay Starr was the number one pop song. The Dow stood at 264 and the median price for a new home in the U.S. was $8,869. A gallon of gas cost 27¢, the average new car $2,409.

My grandfather has recently died, a heart attack. I am named for him and for my great-grandfather, Nathan. Everyone calls me "Harry Nathan" until I grow up, two names as one. It sounds normal to my ears, as natural as "Mary Anne."

I am the third of three children. My parents married early, just before the war, my mother was only eighteen. At twenty-one she gave birth to my brother, at twenty-four to my sister, on the day the war ended in Europe. My mother would tell me she remembered President Truman on the hospital loudspeaker, telling America that the war in Europe was over, just as she was being wheeled into the delivery room to give birth to my sister.

I am born seven years later. There were going to be four children, my mother also once told me, two born early, in her twenties, and two born later, in her thirties. I am born when she is thirty-one.

There is never a fourth child. It would take me thirty years to remember and work out the significance of that.

The family is not particularly well off in 1952, and we are all crowded together. We live with my grandmother in one large apartment.

Upstairs, my great-grandmother, a refugee from Russian pogroms—her twin sister beheaded by a Cossack—lives with two unmarried great-aunts, Naomi and Minnie. Incongruously, the great-aunts make their living running a lingerie shop on Clark Street, in one of Chicago's most run-down neighborhoods (now the center of gay Chicago). Sunday mornings, when my parents and siblings are still asleep, my three-year-old self goes up to the great-aunts, who give me a little coffee with lots of milk.

My uncle, my mother's brother, lives in yet another apartment in the building with his second wife, my jolly Aunt Syl. He's large and silent, but she is my favorite, a boisterous, funny woman, always delighted to see me. She is involved in local Democratic party politics, and one of my earliest memories is everyone gathered around my grandmother's dining room table forging names on nominating petitions, so that Aunt Syl didn't have to go around the neighborhood gathering signatures.

This is, after all, Chicago.

The women dote on me, Aunt Syl, the great aunts, my grandmother, my sister. I am their pet. My sister carries me everywhere, occasionally dropping me. There are so many loving females taking care of me that I don't notice that my mother isn't one of them. Her nose is always stuck in a book.

I don't notice it, that is, until 1957, when we move to the suburbs, like the rest of America. My grandmother and the aunts stayed behind. In the middle of a record-setting Chicago blizzard we moved into a brand new house, and my mother sent me out to play in the snow while she unpacked. The first day the snow was falling so heavily, it was so hard to see, that when I was ready to come inside I went to a neighbor's door by mistake, a door that looked just like ours.

Although none of us realized it at the time, this was the beginning of the end of my family. In eight years, when I am thirteen, there would be a divorce. They waited until just after my Bar Mitzvah.

Doris Lessing has described my parents' and grandparents' generation of Jews (in Britain, though what she says applies to many American Jews as well) as passionate, polemical, clever intellectuals—people who were able to rise above their poverty into the worlds of learning, business, and the arts.

My grandmothers' generation—she, her four sisters and one broth-er—had indeed risen above poverty, the poverty of immigrants. I only knew that side of the family, my mother's side. My father's huge family, a bit longer in the country, was spread out all over the far-away West, and I only met his mother and his brother once or twice. I never met his sister.

That whole side of my family was a mystery to me, and my father enjoyed telling tales about his far-flung relatives. It was a huge family, many children in each generation, so hard to keep track, easy to make up stories or forget or embellish the details. It was said my paternal grandfather, or was it my great-grandfather, owned some worthless land in Wyoming, or was it Montana, then sold it at a loss, a few months before oil was discovered there. My father was born in Nebras-ka but grew up in Los Angeles, when it still had streetcars and the air was clear, he often said with a wistful smile. In Los Angeles my grandfa-ther was said to have been a rabbi, or a labor organizer, or both. There was said to have been a "Hirsch" department store in Berlin before the war to which we were somehow connected, and a gangster in Nevada to whom we were distantly related, or had he moved to Florida? There were cousins in the movie business and an uncle who regularly went fishing with a TV star. When I once asked my father why one of his cousins lived in Helena, he said, deadpan, "He forgot to get off the train." There were relatives in Fargo, in St. Paul, in Phoenix, or had they left Arizona? My great-grandfather was buried in San Francisco. He had many children, there were Hirsches everywhere.

I never knew what to believe about that side of the family, but my mother's family I knew intimately, and their spirit, the spirit that Les-sing describes so well—that cleverness, that love of argument for its own sake, that determination to make it, to rise—was so much a part of me that I never thought about it, never questioned it, never thought life could be lived any other way. *Make something of yourself,* my grand-mother said to me, seriously, amidst the drama of the divorce, when she was the only sane adult around. Ignore the tumult of your parents' crumbling marriage, she was saying, and become your own person.

She didn't need to tell me. The divorce only reinforced a script I had absorbed, memorized, made my own. Make something of yourself. Be smart. Get somewhere.

For my mother and father, life was shaped by the fact that they met just before the war and didn't want to wait, by the fact that they quickly had children. My father had to make a decent living; he didn't have the luxury of contemplating a different kind of life. For my mother, a Jewish woman's role was to keep a proper home (kosher, except in the basement TV room, where we could eat pizza or Chinese food on paper plates), and of course have children—that was what the women in her family did when they got married, and she never wanted anything more. She loved to garden, to cook, to decorate, to read. When my father did finally want to make a change, expand his business, climb higher, it put enormous strain on the marriage.

After the divorce, my father rose again, into the upper-middle class, through his expanding business and his second marriage to a woman with a PhD in English, family money, and a taste for fur. His new wife, briefly a friend to me before she guessed I was gay, was from a rich, Republican, Jewish family in Iowa, a tiny sub-subculture containing so many contradictions it's a wonder their progeny weren't schizophrenic.

My older brother Joel climbed even further than my father through the business world, made it into, or very close, to the wealthy one percent, though he started out wanting to be an American historian and earned fellowships to prestigious graduate schools. He left his PhD program after less than a year, and it was the same story: Early marriage, wanting to start a family, though unlike our parents his marriage has endured for more than fifty years.

My brother was ten years older than I, got married when he was twenty-one and I was only eleven. Although I was only half conscious of it at the time, his dropping out of graduate school a few years later, like my father's story, was for me a cautionary tale.

Do not get sidelined. Decide what you want and go after it. Get where you are going in the world. No matter what.

Make something of yourself.

But in that strange new house in the suburbs, when I was just five and lost in the snow, all this was, of course, in the future. We had gained a foothold in the suburban middle class, but there was a price to be paid, the most profound being the loss of a large, jolly extended family, a family that had sustained my mother and my own youngest self.

In the new house, I am alone for the first time. My father is at work, a longer commute now. My brother, fifteen, is in high school, my sister in junior high; they are blurs as they rush in and out of the house. My mother is working a few days a week in the family business. On the other days, she sits on the new blue couch in the living room and reads. Soon she will be working full time so that my father can undertake a new venture.

There is really only one communal focus for the family, aside from the basic mechanics of meals, clothing, coming and going: being Jewish. My father had studied to be a rabbi, in fact, but was never ordained; this was never explained to us, a bit of a mystery to this day. A crisis of faith? A clash with authority? Simple self-doubt? He never talked about it. He left the seminary and then received a master's degree in social work at the University of Chicago.

My father had studied to be a rabbi. Logic-chopping, a fascination with words and their meaning, argument and debate, a love of books, were in my DNA.

And there was something else. During the Fifties, in homes like ours, the memory of the Holocaust was never far below the surface. Politics weren't just about who got elected but literally, for the adults around me, about life and death. This was never spelled out in words, but it was there unmistakably, in the conversations I overheard, in my father's devotion to newspapers and magazines like *Commentary*. It was there in the books that filled our bookcases, it was there on the Sunday night I was allowed to stay up late to watch the first TV broadcast of *Judgment at Nuremberg*. It was there in our rabbi's sermon on Yom Kippur about the massacre at Babi Yar, the first time I was taken to the adult service.

What I took from all of this, I can now see, what I made my own, was not the specific Jewish way of life, not the 613 commandments, but a more abstract, more visceral concern for justice. I became, eventually, a secular Jew who does not fast on Yom Kippur and who comes close to despising the current, brutal Israeli state. At the same time, almost unconsciously, it seems I absorbed enough of what I observed and what I was taught that I came to share what Susan Sontag labeled Jewish moral seriousness. Sontag wrote in 1964, in her famous "Notes on Camp" that the "two pioneering forces of modern sensibility" were "Jewish moral seriousness and homosexual aestheticism and irony."

The first of these came from my family, in heavy doses.

During the war that helped shape all of this, my father was stationed on the West Coast and was able to get home occasionally to see my mother. So by the time he got out of the army he had a wife and two small children. He finished getting his degrees and then went to work with his father-in-law Harry in a local store selling wallpaper and paint. After we move to the suburbs he is more ambitious, expanding the business from selling to distributing and manufacturing—postwar American capitalism at full throttle. He is traveling to accomplish this, hardly ever around.

No one is around.

So at the age of five, after living in a boisterous extended family, I am suddenly alone. I am quiet, shy, bookish. School becomes my life. In first grade the teacher, Miss Dempster, draws a face in red pencil on our papers, a smiling face with a bowtie (an A), or just a smiling face (B), or face with a mouth in a straight line (C) or a frown (D). I got lots of smiling faces with bowties.

I kept getting them until I had an Ivy League PhD and an Ivy League job.

At home I watch movies, usually alone. My second-grade teacher tells my mother I am too quiet.

Later, I wonder: Was I proto-gay, even then? I used to wonder a lot: *why when how.* It's politically incorrect, now, to wonder *what made me this way?* The question, it is said, implies pathology, which "we" reject, and in truth I don't much care, haven't for a long time.

But I used to. When and how did this happen, this difference? In the middle-class, suburban, Midwestern world of the 1950s, it was pathology, not mere difference. And despite my firm conscious rejection of that version of the world, despite my years of supportive therapy, despite my determined and finally joyful embrace of all things gay, despite all the gay freedom day parades in which I have marched, on both coasts, despite my turning even my academic life in a gay direction—despite all this, over so many years, that question never entirely disappears.

When why how.

Hard questions when they first appear.

After the divorce, my mother and I moved into a small apartment. It was not home; home was gone. My brother was finished with college, married, busy, starting on a career. My sister was finishing school and would also soon be married. Both parents remarried as well, quickly, and relations with both step-parents soon would be fraught.

Neither new parental marriage had much room for me. I was a remnant, a reminder of a family that was gone, like the house.

* * *

A sage once said: *You live if you learn to dance to the music that ails you.*

Learning to dance.

I have never been athletic, bodily grace is not in my repertoire, but I did learn to dance, little by little, step by awkward step, easiest dances first, later the harder steps. I began dancing through books; that came naturally. I danced in libraries, in classes, later in large lecture halls in the Midwest and in small seminar rooms in the Ivy League. I danced by putting words on paper.

I began to dance as I shed the closet, small steps at first, very small. A brief, trembling foray at twenty-one to the one gay bar in Ann Arbor. Not correcting the impressions of my closest friends in graduate school when they guessed. At twenty-five walking to the corner drugstore on arriving in Boston to buy, for the first time, *Gay Community News*, my heart pounding. It was a signal moment in my life when the nice older woman behind the cash register, from whom I got my prescriptions, didn't so much as blink.

Coming out to some of my junior colleagues at Harvard, and letting the rest guess. When you are unmarried and unattached by age thirty, when you never bring a date, even the most obtuse, if they are around your own age, can figure things out. Older, more senior colleagues at Harvard never discussed it, of course. That would be rude. They never asked questions; questions would break the code. They never discussed the other gay man amongst them, much older, not married, a full professor close to retirement. His classification: *Not the marrying kind.*

Those Victorian manners suited me in the Ivy League, served me well with my advisors at Princeton and my distinguished senior colleagues at Harvard. Even when I ran into that one senior professor at a Cambridge gay bar and we became friendly, he and I never discussed it. We chatted amiably at the bar about other things, as if we had run into each other at an art exhibit.

Gentlemen did not discuss their personal lives. No, of course not, that would not be polite, that was not the way things are done.

That gave me space.

By the time I reached California, in my mid-thirties, everyone knew, and there was no need to pretend or proclaim. And in the warm sun of California, where walking around half-naked was standard practice and discretion was a strange custom from a foreign land, I even found ways of choreographing my own ballet, my private life and my professional life coming together as I pursued gay projects on and off campus. I became known.

It takes half a lifetime, sometimes, to find what you are looking for, to learn the right steps. To get away. To hear the music and dance.

3
GEOGRAPHY 101

I *will find it somewhere else.*

But where?

Ann Arbor in the early Seventies, marijuana everywhere. The Princeton campus, magnolias in the spring. The manuscript reading room of the Library of Congress, the papers of a Supreme Court Justice. The press room in Richard Nixon's White House, an intern for the *New York Times*, long before Washington interns produced scandal. Harvard Square. Southern California.

Libraries. Northwestern's beautiful new library overlooking Lake Michigan, sneaking in while still in high school, pretending to be in college. The appropriately named UGLI, Ann Arbor, coffee from a machine in the basement, where friends congregate. (I am still in touch with some of those basement friends. Not too long along ago I spoke to one of them about the death of her father.) Then Firestone, named like many buildings at Princeton for a wealthy corporate family; a carrel shared with an undergraduate (again in the basement). In Cambridge, Widener and the Harvard Law Library, old, hushed. La Jolla, a branch of the University of California, a multi-layered, odd-shaped spaceship, all glass and steel floating above the ocean.

Cafes in which to read. Pamplona in Cambridge. Quel Fromage, Hillcrest, San Diego, before it turned into a Thai restaurant. Coffee News, St. Paul. Paris, every street corner.

Where is the toy store for you, a therapist once asked me. The answer came immediately: Bookstores. Kroch's and Brentano's, the Loop, high school summer job; the first place I went, and they hired

21

me. The original Borders, Ann Arbor. Cambridge, so many, open late. Gaglignani, Paris. Provincetown Bookshop, "books to tickle your fancy." Amazon.com.

Even before I could read books, long before, I would play with them. I would take one down from the bookshelf and hold it, pretend to read it, carry it around. My parents gave me that attachment; they would come home from work, we would have dinner, and they would read. They were tired, exhausted, often, from the businesses they ran and endured but never loved . . . but never too tired to read. People of the book.

First grade, the workbooks, with teacher's instructions printed in small print along the periphery of the page. The class struggled with "See Spot Run." I read the teacher's instructions. "Choose one student to read this page aloud." I raise my hand.

Kept for forty years, carted from one coast to the other and then back to the Midwest, books from my first year at college, Introduction to Sociology, European History, Introduction to Philosophy, Cultural Anthropology, until a flood in the basement of my house in Oberlin damaged them beyond repair.

Rivers. The Charles. The Seine. Oceans and beaches. Ogunquit, Maine. Herring Cove, Provincetown. Coronado in San Diego, reading thick library books while the tanned, perfect bodies played volleyball around me . . . night-blooming jasmine, endless summer.

Snow. Chicago, Michigan, Boston, then escape, then back, rural Ohio. A friend asks, what is your greatest pleasure in life, where are you then? Reading in front of the fire, I say. With winter horse's hooves on the cobblestone, Beacon Hill, mounted policemen, still riding in the early Eighties. Then in St. Paul, reading by the fire with Patsy, my golden retriever, at my feet.

Borders. The Ivy League versus the rest of the world. Southern California versus Northern California, one kind of border; the whole state versus the rest, another . . . a different country, though passports are not required. San Diego versus Tijuana, an invisible line on the ground, no physical boundary at all, no river, no mountain. Take a trolley and then walk across the border, and suddenly you're in the third world, just a few short miles from some of the most expensive real estate on the planet.

The Mississippi River, dividing St Paul from Minneapolis. "Can you see across it?" a friend, who has never set foot outside Manhattan, asks me. "Yes, you can see across it," I assure her, stifling a laugh. You can even walk across one of the many bridges, though in winter, which is most of the year, the wind is fierce.

The invisible border between "A" list scholars and everyone else, between elite institutions and the rest, between universities and colleges.

Some borders easier to cross than others.

Colleagues. Judith Shklar. Judith Halberstam. Mentors. Reading groups. Students . . . lawyers, writers, teachers. Titles. Preceptor. Professor. Head Tutor. Dean (briefly, a disaster). Hundreds of students in a lecture hall, microphone in my hand. Four in a graduate seminar.

The search. Knowledge. Connection. The right script. The right place.

4
POLITICS 201

Spring 1970, senior year of high school. Waiting for colleges to accept or reject and taking advanced placement tests.

I edit the yearbook, and, for the first time, we introduce commentary on national politics into the book. We include quotes in the opening section from Coretta Scott King and others, and pictures contrasting the frivolity of high school life with what is happening in the outside world. We include a picture of a child starving in Appalachia, pictures of soldiers marching through the mud and being ambushed in Vietnam. "It's not often when the outside world confronts us," I write in the yearbook's opening passage, "but it does happen every now and then." I write of "the disturbing knowledge that there is another world beside our own, a world in which we become minute and alone." The book's theme is contrast—antithesis, we call it—and to make the point the pictures are all black and white, no color at all.

There are a few complaints about the yearbook, from students, from parents. There are dirty looks in the hallway. I am yelled at on the school bus. My co-editor is briefly in tears. The principal takes heat from the community about allowing us to be so political, but he defends us, an early lesson in free speech.

I am shaken by the response, a bit frightened that someone, one of the varsity athletes, might slug me or trash the yearbook's offices, but mixed in with the fear is something else, something new. I am afraid but I am also . . . resolute. Glad to have stirred things up. To my great surprise, there is a kind of pleasure mixed in with the fear. I have taken a stand, and I am . . . proud. A bit defiant. I see for the first time that there is a price to be paid for speaking out, and I think . . . ok.

The national and international news that season seemed to justify our approach, and we felt, in some cosmic manner, vindicated. President Nixon told the nation on April 20 that the war in Vietnam was winding down.

One of his many lies.

On April 30 U.S. troops invaded Cambodia, and the invasion did not go well. Protests erupt around the world. On May 1 a nationwide student strike was called; hundreds of college campuses shut down. Marches, rallies, headlines, chaos.

On May 4, the fourth day of protest, the Ohio National Guard shoots four unarmed students at Kent State University and wounds nine others. It seems the victims were shot in the back or from a significant distance. Two of the four were protesting the invasion and war. Two of the four were just walking from class to class.

Shot in the back. From a significant distance.

Ohio governor Jim Rhodes, just before the shooting, spoke angrily about the need to "eradicate" the protest.

Protests, strikes, outrage spread and deepen everywhere. Students demonstrate in Montreal, Calcutta, Caracas, Canberra. From the Vatican the Pope denounces the escalation of the war. In the U.S., protests take place on more than 80 percent of the nation's college campuses, with 500 of them shut down by strikes. Four million students participate.

Four million.

There is a picture, a famous picture, printed everywhere, of a young girl—a fourteen-year-old runaway named Mary Ann Vecchio, it later turned out—crouching next to the dead body of Jeffrey Miller, a student at Kent State. Mary Ann is lifting up her arms in shock and rage and grief. Another image seared into the brain, into many young brains that horrible week at the beginning of a new decade.

The picture won a Pulitzer.

At our high school, my friends and I have one foot out the door, but we go to a meeting after school, try to figure out if there is anything we puny high school students can do. My friend Sharon has drafted a letter demanding accountability, addressed to President Nixon. I suggest we gather signatures, turn the letter into a petition. We are frightened but we do it. Trembling, we mail the petition to the White House, with our names prominently displayed as the organizers. Sharon and I attend a rally at nearby Northwestern University, where hordes of policemen watch the crowd warily. Everyone seems frightened of the police but the dominant emotions are determination and anger, resolute anger.

Four dead.

They were peacefully protesting on a college campus. None of them armed with any weapon more dangerous than a textbook, or closer than 265 feet to the Guardsmen who shot them, supposedly in self-defense.

I had just recently heard a tape of Fannie Lou Hamer addressing the Democratic National Convention in 1964, protesting the all-white delegation to that convention from Mississippi. "Is this America?" Fannie asks the Democrats, taunting. "I question America," Fannie, born dirt poor in the Jim Crow South, lectures the establishment Democrats. The party in Mississippi had split over the question of race, and Fanny, representing one side, has come to challenge the national leaders who have tolerated racial discrimination in its Southern wing. "Is this America, the land of the free and the home of the brave?" As we gather signatures on our petition after Kent State and watch the news and try to figure out why the world has gone insane, I hear Fannie's clear, strong voice, replaying in my head like a stuck record.

"I question America," Fannie said.

No one who heard Fannie speak could ever forget the sound of her voice. Historians still write about her.

Is this America?

From a significant distance.

Walking from class to class, something I would be doing on a college campus in a few short months. Someone hangs a banner out a window at NYU: "They can't kill us all."

In Manhattan, construction workers go on a rampage, attacking protestors, while the police stand by and do nothing—all duly filmed, shown on the evening news. I feel a rush of panic as I watch the tape on the news, as I see a phalanx of hardhats charging toward the protestors like an army, then beating the ones who could not get away. It was all filmed from above, so what was happening was crystal clear.

Unprovoked attack.

Another image seared into my brain, a brain by now overloaded with images that could not be forgotten, or even fully absorbed, much less understood.

Watching that scene on that tape, the action filmed from above, it felt like I was watching something break, irretrievably shatter, something that would not be put back together, not within my lifetime. Red and blue America were born over those few days in May, 1970, as I tried to concentrate on my Advanced Placement exams.

It felt as if the mere holding of a political opinion was dangerous.

It felt like the world was drenched in blood.

They can't kill us all.

* * *

Ann Arbor, the fall of 1970, the University of Michigan. Chosen in part because it was cheap in those days, even for out-of-state students, because it was supposed to be a good school, whatever that meant, and above all because it was a politicized and radical campus—the birthplace of SDS, a place that held early teach-ins on Vietnam, on the environment, on Black Power—a place at the center of Sixties politics and culture.

My father drove me to campus from Chicago on a weekend in late August. It was hot, Midwestern hot and muggy. Students were walking around wearing as little as possible. As we drove through town, we saw some Hare Krishnas dancing on a street corner. "What's that?" my father asked. "People," I responded, and smiled at him. He was taken aback, slightly appalled. I was glad that he was appalled, glad to see at least this small example of difference between us. I wanted to leave my family, my suburb, the Jewish middle class, all of my sheltered youth, behind.

My father did not like to waste time and needed to get back to work early Monday morning. We stayed in a motel Saturday night and he dropped me off at my dorm Sunday morning at 8:00 a.m., the very first moment it was possible to check in. He was convinced there would be a crowd, confusion, delays, and he was irritable, anxious. But at 8:00 a.m. Sunday morning I was the only person there. I got the key from a janitor and we carried my suitcases and boxes through empty corridors.

We said our goodbyes, and he left me in my small room with bunk beds on the top floor of Mosher-Jordan, one of the smaller dorms.

There was perfect silence, stillness.

I felt for a moment as if I did not exist.

I unpacked. Out the window I saw an empty playing field and buildings in the distance, some brand new, some very old. I did not yet know what they contained. I wandered around but there was no sign of life in the dorm, no sign of the roommate to whom I had been assigned or anyone else. I took a shower, then studied the campus map on the bulletin board in the hallway.

I felt very still, very calm, as I always do at significant or difficult moments. I walked to the center of town, sweating again in the heat, had lunch alone in a small restaurant—meals had not yet started in the dorm—and watched the other students eating alone or in groups of two or three or four. I looked at the books they were carrying, caught snatches of conversation. Someone mentioned "Che," and I did not know who "Che" was.

I wondered what the rest of my life would be like.

* * *

Orientation. In the evening there is an optional "encounter group" (this is, after all, 1970). I am intrigued, a little frightened, but I go. We are first instructed to pair up with someone we haven't yet met and tell each other "what messages we convey by our appearance, before we say anything." I think this is weird but I'm game, and didn't I come to college to have new experiences?

The young man with whom I pair up had long blonde hair and looked like a surfer from California, I told him. He looked carefree and happy, and was, I speculated, a musician.

He was from Detroit, he told me, and had had a nervous breakdown, losing a year between high school and college, recuperating, including a long stint in a mental hospital. He's not musical at all and has decided to study medicine and psychiatry.

He tells me I look shy and serious, that I came to college to learn, that I have a few close friends but not a lot of casual acquaintances, that I don't do drugs, and that I will end up a writer or a professor.

Oh my.

I'm completely wrong about him, but he's exactly right about me; apparently I'm an open book. The encounter group ends and people begin to smoke joints, and I pass. My blonde partner smiles as I get up to leave.

Is being serious a bad thing, I wonder? I had been a bit of an outcast in high school—not a jock, not cool—would I now be in the same boat because I was "serious" and didn't do drugs? What does this mean, all this getting high, something that held very little interest for me? For drugs were everywhere in Ann Arbor in the early Seventies, mostly marijuana—dope, everyone called it—common as coffee and beer. The halls of the dorms reeked of it as soon as other students arrived, and the first major decision of my new, quasi-adult life would be whether I would join in.

The issue kept coming up, everywhere, at every gathering of students in the dorm, everywhere I went on campus. My fellow students were giddy with freedom, getting high and hooking up.

I was lost. I hadn't come to college to get high or hook up. I wondered if I had made a terrible mistake, if I had chosen the wrong school. I needed distraction, needed desperately to fit in somewhere, so soon after the encounter group I went to the offices of the campus newspaper to see about joining—I had been a high school journalist, editing the yearbook, working on the student newspaper, taking summer courses at Northwestern's journalism school.

The Michigan Daily was a nationally known college paper. Tom Hayden had been editor a decade earlier. It had its own campus building with an old-fashioned printing press in the basement, and—it loved to point out to people—it had perhaps the last five-cent Coke machine in the country. New recruits were told just to show up late afternoons and evenings, hang around, meet people, begin to get a sense of how the paper worked. So I went and dutifully hung around.

Nothing happened, at least not to me. To my shock, no one wanted to talk much about what was happening outside Ann Arbor. There were a couple of other recruits there, one boy and one girl, who flirted endlessly with older staff members, had their hands all over them. They were assigned stories to write; I wasn't.

This is interesting,

I wrote in my journal.

Journalism is now sex. No sex, no story??

In the evening the atmosphere became party-like, and joints were passed around; the rolling paper was kept in a file cabinet marked "coffee supplies," and there was lots of making out in corners. An older, friendly reporter, sensing my discomfort, pulled me aside. "Maybe think about joining the business staff," he said.

Like the aftermath of the encounter group, this was a lesson that would be repeated during all four of my years in Ann Arbor. For many of my fellow students, "politics," more and more, meant lifestyle. "Radical" meant radical living—or at least a kind of living seemingly different from what we had come from. Caring about or understanding what was happening in the world was increasingly optional. People were reflexively opposed to what everyone called The Establishment, wanted the war in Vietnam to end, hated Nixon, but most didn't really want to go much deeper. By 1970 in Ann Arbor, the hope and energy of mid-Sixties radicalism had largely turned to despair, or indifference; the real political energy had been spent. SDS had imploded. The campus had been torn apart not only over the war and Kent State but over racial issues as well, and race divided the student body in a way opposition to the war had not. Most wanted to turn away from complex, divisive subjects and political talk.

Sex and drugs and rock and roll were what many wanted, and Ann Arbor gave them copious amounts. The counterculture was in full bloom.

What none of us stopped to think about was what all of this meant, what the counterculture was really about—for this deluge of sex and drugs in the late Sixties and early Seventies was in crucial ways an extension of the consumer ethic of postwar America, and rested on a prosperity that was about to come to a crashing halt. The world had never seen widespread economic growth and stability of the kind on display in the United States in the thirty years after 1945. It was a golden age, the age of the American middle class. We college students thought ourselves rebels, but we were, in many ways, children of our time, enjoying our leisure and pursuing more and more of what gave us pleasure. For our parents it was a suburban house and air conditioning, martinis perhaps, two cars, stereos, *Playboy* and *Good Housekeeping*. For their children it was sex and dope at relatively affordable state universities in places like Ann Arbor, Berkeley, Madison.

Sex and dope and, for a brief moment, politics.

We were, in some fundamental way, innocent, having ridden the wave of post-war prosperity to a university education. We did not know that the good years would end the moment we finished college, that upward mobility would become more difficult, that what was coming was an oil embargo, inflation and sky-high interest rates, a resurgent rightwing and Ronald Reagan. We did not know that the cheap walk-up apartments in Boston and Manhattan and San Francisco into which we moved when we finished school would soon be converted into expensive lofts and condos and townhouses. We did not know that in about ten years some of us would start dying from a mysterious plague.

All that would have seemed impossible, insane if you had told us about it in the fall of 1970 in Ann Arbor. Life was easy, tuition was low, and sex and dope and rock and roll were there for the taking.

I was not aware of any of this at the time, of course. What I noticed, though, was that what I thought of as real politics, in my overly serious way, seemed to have faded. The war dragged on and Nixon was still president. All the marching, all the rallies seemed by now like wasted energy, pointless. The hard slog of activism had lost its appeal. In its place there were day-to-day pleasures and the need to do well in school, to think about one's future—the beginnings of what Yale president Kingman Brewster would eventually label grim careerism. Of the six people who would become my housemates, two became doctors, one a lawyer, one a New York writer for an advertising journal, one a New York–based artist's agent. And then, of course, there was me, who quickly went off to graduate school. Of the seven of us, only one chose a different, non-professional life, staying in Ann Arbor, staying stoned, dabbling in this or that. Among most of our mutual friends the story was the same—a brief countercultural adventure in college before facing the real world.

Take away the long hair and the drugs, and conventional careerism was everywhere—the Me Decade was well on its way. It shocked me when the editor of the *Daily* my first year took a job at the *Wall Street Journal* after he graduated, but I was no longer shocked or even surprised when a few years later some of my hippest, most counter-cultural classmates marched off to business school or to jobs on Madison Avenue, at IBM, at the Chase Manhattan Bank.

Much later, when I taught a course about American political thought in the Sixties and Seventies, I realized I had arrived in Ann

Arbor five to ten years too late. The earnestness of the early and mid-Sixties—civil rights marches, early SDS—would have suited me, for I was nothing if not earnest. I didn't think politics was about getting high. To me, it was about figuring out who profited from the war in Vietnam, and why it didn't end, since public opinion in the country had so clearly turned against it. It wasn't about having lots of sex, but about why there were so few female professors—I had one in four years, and she was a temporary lecturer, not a professor—and why there were women's bathrooms only on every other floor of some of the faculty office buildings. Politics to me wasn't about long hair—though I dutifully grew a beard—it was about why Detroit, forty minutes away—where hordes of my fellow students lived in safe, all-white suburbs—was a dying city. I had nothing against long hair or getting high or people who wanted to have sex; I saw the narrowness of middle-class respectability, the blandness and insulation of the suburbs from which we had come, as much as anyone. But at the time, I didn't think any of these things meant very much in the grand scheme of things.

I hungered to understand the grand scheme of things.

I wanted the real story. For some of us—the most earnest, perhaps, or the most frightened, the misfits—politics was more than a college fashion.

For decades I have been unable to decide if we were the lucky ones, or fools.

At the time, I was eager to fit in, so I grew that beard and drank a fair amount of cheap wine, which made me funny and a bit loose, but still in control. I tried marijuana a few times, spent the next day feeling hung-over each time, and didn't like the feeling at all. I couldn't read, couldn't focus. The blonde psychiatrist was dead right—I was an eternal student, in school to learn. Getting stoned got in the way.

And, oh yes. There was one more thing. It's easy now to see that I was afraid of drugs because I was afraid of losing control, of letting my attraction to men reveal itself, afraid that stoned I would tell the blonde psychiatrist that he was hot, or make a pass, or even stare at him a little too intently, or tell the female *Daily* editor who put her hand on my leg one evening that I wasn't interested.

I wasn't ready to lose control, to be discovered, *known*. I wasn't yet convinced that sexual freedom mattered—how could it, when to exercise it would be to ostracize myself? I didn't yet know that the personal was political, something that now everyone holds as fundamental, almost banal truth.

For this was 1970 in the Midwest. Second-wave feminism and gay liberation were just beginning to analyze sex. Feminists were everywhere in Ann Arbor, but the gay community was still hiding, mostly ashamed. That would change rapidly in a few years, as it was already changing on the coasts, but at that moment in that place it felt like there was no space to explore being gay, no role other than outcast available to those who were out.

I wanted in, not out. For the moment, that meant ignoring sex as much as possible.

Later, I thought. Later. I will deal with that later.

Un-stoned and in the closet, I still made very good friends—lifelong friends, some of them. And, looking for distraction, I began to take advantage of Ann Arbor's cultural offerings, which were ample and, if they cost anything, amazingly cheap. Martha Graham's dance company. The Cleveland Orchestra. Marcel Marceau, the famous mime. Helen Hayes touring in the Broadway company of *Harvey*. Concerts by Joan Baez and Joni Mitchell, lectures by radical attorney William Kunstler and aging Supreme Court Justice William O. Douglas. Endless films— one could find something interesting to do every night.

Mostly, though, I threw myself into classes—never underestimate the power of sublimation, a friend later said to me when I described my time in college. Classes meant, at the beginning, large lectures with small discussion sections taught by graduate students. My freshman year I took social science and humanities classes— anthropology, sociology, history, philosophy, political science—and loved them all. Marx, John Stuart Mill, primitive tribes in South America, chivalry in medieval Europe, the industrial revolution, party identification and voting. It was all enticing, fascinating. I couldn't get enough.

Michigan is huge, and lectures in introductory classes were in large auditoriums or amphitheaters. The professor stood on stage and talked into a microphone. This was long before PowerPoint; most of the time there was nothing but the professor's voice—no diagrams, no handouts. Most professors didn't even use the blackboard.

My very first lecture was Cultural Anthropology, Conrad Kottak, young and handsome with a hip demeanor. He had just returned from studying a fierce tribe in Brazil and was very tan. There were large "no smoking" signs but he lit a cigarette while looking over his notes as students took their seats. When it was time to start the lecture he stomped on his cigarette in a gesture so exaggerated it seemed like a choreographed ballet step.

Later in the morning History 101, European History before the French Revolution. Another young professor, James Allen Vann III, with elegant speech and a genteel Southern accent. He managed to communicate through his Ivy League manners and clothes—tweed jacket and vest in early September, despite the heat—that he had no idea how he ended up in the Midwest. Incongruously, that class took place in a science building, and Professor Vann looked skeptical as he entered and surveyed the lab table at the front of the auditorium. There was a fuss with the teaching fellows as he sent them scurrying to find a small lecturn he could place on top of the table.

As I flitted from one humanities and social science course to another that year, enjoying them all, I felt a bit like Rosalind Russell in *Auntie Mame*—"life is a banquet, and most poor suckers are starving to death." I was ready. I listened. I was a sponge.

* * *

Sunday afternoon, late October, the dorm's lounge. On weekday evenings and Sunday nights, the lounge is full of people studying, but it's 2:00 in the afternoon, the sun is shining, the temperature is near seventy—Indian summer. Everyone can feel that winter is coming fast; there have already been snow flurries though nothing has stuck to the ground. Everyone is out grabbing a last bit sun before the long winter sets in.

Nearly everyone.

I sit in the lounge reading, taking notes. The lounge is deserted. It doesn't even cross my mind that this is in any way strange or unusual until Barb, who lives on my hall, passes by the lounge, sees me, stops and says "What the hell are you doing?"

"Reading."

"Come outside."

"No, I want to finish this."

"You realize no one in Ann Arbor is working right now, don't you?"

I look up. "Actually there are six of us. The other five are graduate students." She laughs, shakes her head, and leaves.

For a moment I think she's right, I should run after her, but then I look down at the book I'm holding—the writings of the young Marx, a book that still sits on my shelf—and I think, no.

And then, something strange, after I am alone again in the empty lounge. An image comes to me, of my mother sitting on a similar couch, before the divorce, reading, always reading, and of me, age six or seven, trying to get her attention, without much success. And in the next split second the image of my father reading, every night reading in bed before going to sleep.

That marriage, that life, that house are long gone now, but I see that I am still living there, that I really am their child, and I am startled, perhaps more startled than I have ever been. I had been feeling very glad these first months of college to be away from my family, to be rid of them in some fundamental way, but I see now they are not gone, not gone at all.

I smile what I imagine is a rueful smile, hear myself take a very deep breath, and I go back to the young Marx.

* * *

I read everything I could get my hands on, all the required reading in every course, sometimes all the recommended reading and even more background, related material on my own. I became a habitué of the bookshops . . . I was always reading. Like the title character of John Williams's academic novel *Stoner*, I had fallen in love with the idea of a university.

In Philosophy we read some of Marx; I read much more. For my class on European history I did background reading on the French Revolution and the Revolutions of 1848. In Introduction to Sociology I read an analysis of modern American marriage and a critique of the idea that "men and women marry because they are in love." Not quite so, it seems. "If one investigated a little further into the behavior that is engaged in prior to marriage under the misleading euphemism of 'courtship,' one finds channels of interaction that are often rigid to the point of ritual." I read about unspoken assumptions, the importance of class, frames of reference. In Introduction to Anthropology I listened to a lecture about a primitive tribe in which an adolescent male was re-quired to have sex with an older male, as a rite of passage, even if he went on to live an entirely heterosexual life.

Channels of interaction. Frames of reference. Customs, roles, class. The world was tilting. I wasn't in the suburbs any longer.

* * *

February, 1971, second semester. I am taking a course on Shakespeare. Friday night, temperature well below zero, more than a foot of fresh snow on the ground. I eat the dorm's mystery meat early and then trudge off to the library, wrapped in my new down jacket. There is hardly a soul on the sidewalks, very few at the library.

I need to start reading *King Lear*. The professor has put on reserve recordings of the plays, and he suggests listening while reading. This is long before personal computers. To listen to the recordings one has to go to the audio lab.

It's a very long play. I assume I'll listen to the first act or two, perhaps for an hour or so, then go down to the coffee room, look for someone to talk to, maybe we'll go to a late movie at one of the film societies, as we often did.

I sit at a carrel, surrounded by pegboard. I put on the headphones. Paul Scofield is Lear, Vanessa Redgrave is Cordelia. The text is in front of me. I see nothing but the text and the blank pegboard, I hear nothing but the recording, the voices trapped in the overwhelming tragedy, the irony, the betrayal, the madness.

Nearly four hours later, the play ends. I am sobbing, bathed in sweat. My bladder is bursting but I have not moved. I look up at the clock and see that it is after 11:00; for a moment I do not know if it is AM or PM. I look out the window, see dark and snow. Ah yes. Nighttime. PM. I'm in Ann Arbor, Michigan. February. I'm a college student. This was an assignment.

I am sobbing so loudly the clerk behind the desk comes and asks me if I am all right. "I don't know," I say. I do not know exactly what I feel but I know something has happened to me.

* * *

Forty years later, now a professor at Oberlin. The last class, when I tell students I will reveal the meaning of life, let them ask any question they like. A young woman, an advisee, asks me, "What was the formative experience of your undergraduate career?" *King Lear* I say, before I have time to think about an answer. I tell the story. And after the class where I tell the story for the first time, I understand what I encountered that cold January night in Ann Arbor. The brute strength of words. For me it will become the power of true words, words about the world, about my country, torn apart as I became an adult, but it was there for me that cold night at the library.

* * *

I got a B+ in that Shakespeare course (I wrote a confused essay about *The Merchant of Venice*), but in all my other classes my freshman year I got As, which I used to talk my way into the honors program. I had not been admitted into it when I was accepted into the freshman class, which rankled, and which I didn't understand. Later I learned it was because my combined SAT score was a tad on the low side. The honors program meant discussion sections in large classes taught by the professor, not a graduate student, and it meant small seminars in the junior year. I wanted in.

So, after getting my four As first semester, I made an appointment to see the director, a humanities professor straight out of Hollywood casting: round face, sweater vest, tweed jacket with elbow patches, a deep voice, and a pipe. Uncle Otto, everyone called him, from the German department. He asked me what books I had read in the past six months that had not been required in a class.

I smiled, and started rattling off a list. He stopped me, nodded, and asked a few perfunctory questions—likely major, where I was from— then told me to make an appointment with one of the advisors.

* * *

I chose political science as my major, history as my minor. History courses were lecture courses, and I was dazzled by Gerald Linderman, tall, distinguished-looking American historian, who gave elegant, beautifully crafted lectures about America in the late nineteenth and early twentieth centuries. He seamlessly worked into his lectures the occasional comment about current events, about the war in Vietnam, as well as humor, and his humor was as elegant as his analysis. Could I ever speak so clearly, present an argument so nuanced, I wondered? If this is what it means to be a professor, well then . . . the idea began to percolate.

History was familiar to me from high school, and it seemed the likeliest choice as a major. But then one day I overheard a conversation between two other honor students while waiting to see one of the advisors.

"What are you gonna major in?"

"History."

"Oh come on Frank, history majors are a dime a dozen."

It was something I had often heard, and it worried me. Of course every major attracted hordes of students on campuses like Michigan—there were 15,000 undergraduates, after all—but that didn't occur to me at the time. I started thinking maybe political science was a more esoteric, more personal, more practical choice. No one I knew was thinking about it as a major, and it would be good background for journalism, high on my list of possible careers.

And political science was entirely new to me, and, at the time, dazzling. Why won't Congress end the war in Vietnam? We can explain that, political scientists seemed to be saying. We have a theory. Why do so few people vote? We can explain that, we have a theory. Why is crime soaring and cities like Detroit dying? We can explain that, we have a theory.

I was seduced. I was smitten.

I declared my major, studied hard and watched what was happening in the world with a combination of dread, fascination, and horror. I read nearly every issue of the *New York Times* a day late in the reading room of the library. I watched the CBS Evening News.

In the spring of my freshman year the Weather Underground—the tiny, violent remnant of SDS—bombed offices at the U.S. Capitol. In May, 70,000 people gathered in Washington for an antiwar demonstration. That summer, the *New York Times* and the *Washington Post* began publishing the Pentagon Papers. Even my much more conservative brother, with whom I was staying for a while in Washington, was horrified by the first Papers, which detailed the unending government stupidity and duplicity since the 1950s that had gotten us mired in Vietnam. The Papers—a leaked official Defense Department history of the war—made clear, among many other things, that LBJ had blatantly lied, over and over again, to both Congress and the public, as he dramatically escalated the war in the mid-Sixties. Thousands had died and were dying still, billions were being spent, and it was all a mistake, a mistake based on lies, American hubris at its worst.

The war seemed to hang over everything else, as it had in high school, and it was not merely an abstraction. We cared about it so deeply because there was still a draft. Like many, I was determined not to fight. I decided that, if called, I would request classification as a conscientious objector, which would have meant duty as a medic, perhaps, or a desk job.

With trepidation, heart pounding, I visited one of the local draft counseling centers, which was in the basement of a local Protestant church. I had never set foot inside a church, and, as I walked in, I felt a bit like Dorothy landing in Oz. As I made my way to the basement, I muttered what had become a generational tag line: "Toto, we're not in Kansas anymore."

The draft counselor was a boyish, strikingly handsome, older minister, a representative of the species referred to by my mother as PAWs, Protestants Aging Well. He asked me what my religious background was.

"Very Jewish."

"Too bad," he said with a laugh, meaning it as a joke.

"You're telling me," I replied.

Until recently, one could gain classification as a CO only if one were a member of a pacifist denomination, such as the Quakers, and that was still the easiest path. But a few years prior, the minister told me, the Supreme Court had broadly interpreted the draft law to allow CO status for those whose views on war derived from a "sincere and meaningful belief," a belief "which occupies in the life of its possessor a place parallel to that filled by the God" of those who had routinely gotten the exemption. The kind, handsome minister helped me make my case, and I filed the necessary papers. I also made a mental note to learn something about the Supreme Court.

"What have you learned about humanity?" the minister asked me. "Write down your thoughts about that."

I went back to my dorm and wrote it down. What I had been learning in all those social science classes came pouring out of me, and the theme seemed to be cultural and historical relativism—how could one know, even in a war, which side was really right and which was wrong, who was the real enemy.

Writing and filing my CO papers had a lasting effect on me. It reinforced the reality I had only seen at a distance—that politics really could be a matter of life and death—at the moment, my own. I didn't know if I was a coward for not wanting to fight or brave for refusing—I suspected the former—but one thing was clear. It made me more determined than ever to understand what was happening in the world.

I tried not to think about what I would do if they refused me CO status and I was drafted—Canada? Jail? Luckily, my number was never called.

Meanwhile, the news seemed to supply an endless stream of confusion and significance. In September, at the beginning of my sophomore year, prisoners rioted at Attica. The California Supreme Court abolished the death penalty. Early in the spring of 1972, Nixon went to China, and Angela Davis went on trial. Altogether it felt like the world was speeded up, out of control, headed over a cliff. At times the news was too much to absorb, much less understand. Nixon, the red-baiter, in China? Angela Davis, a young professor of philosophy at UCLA, put on trial for murder?

There was an obvious place to be if I wanted to go deeper, understand more: Washington. The University had one of the first college summer internship programs in the country, and I got accepted for an unpaid slot at the local NBC station. Off I went to follow reporters and camera crews around in Washington's thick summer heat to see how the news got manufactured.

Although I worked for local reporters, "local" in this context was Washington, and the stories I observed were sometimes of national significance—a new recruiting policy in the army; an interview with George McGovern, the Democratic presidential nominee that year, about possible home rule for the District of Columbia; the trial of Arthur Bremer, who had shot George Wallace in a nearby Maryland town when Wallace was running his racist campaign for President in 1968. I attended Bremer's trial, mingled with reporters from all over the country and a few from overseas, observed the cozy, off-the-record relationship between reporters and the prosecutor's office, saw how reporters shared information and sometimes didn't bother to check their facts. On other stories I got to see how the White House press operated and how reporters developed relationships at City Hall or with members of Congress. I watched as Washington's mayor propositioned the female reporter I was working with that day, half in jest. Occasionally a reporter would talk a story over with me, let me do background research, or let me draft a bit of copy to be read on the air.

That summer the first edition of *Ms.* Magazine was published and much discussed, and perhaps the most eye-opening experience of the summer was observing the extraordinary sexism of the mostly male reporters and staff. Behavior that today would trigger lawsuits was routine. *Relentless heterosexuality* I called it in my journal, and it was constant. The camera crews ogling and bothering women on the street, the head film editor berating a young woman who worked for him; a steady stream of comments about how women looked from almost every male in the building, from the managing editor to the video techs. Women reporters who got ahead were assumed to have slept their way to their jobs, and the sexual banter never ended. There was much discussion about a gay reporter who had been fired, apparently just for being gay. The word was never spoken, but the facts were clear and, to me, ominous. I was glad to have spent a summer there but I wasn't sure TV news was for me.

When I returned to Michigan in the fall of 1972, the big news was the election: McGovern's crushing defeat by Nixon—which felt inexplicable in the little island of Ann Arbor—and then, soon after, the beginnings of Watergate—the third rate burglary, in Nixon's memorable phrase, that led to a constitutional crisis and his downfall.

A janitor at the Watergate complex, an office building in D.C., discovered something vaguely suspicious one night, which led to the discovery of burglars at the headquarters of the Democratic National Committee. The burglars were eventually tied to Nixon's reelection committee. The President and his henchmen then attempted to cover up the crime, and that included hush money. Little by little the press hacked away at Nixon and those around him until he faced certain impeachment. The drama unfolded step by inexorable step, over several years, and was a bit like watching a fatal accident in slow motion. My junior year also brought the Supreme Court's decision in *Roe v. Wade* and the signing of the Paris Peace Accords, finally ending the war. At the end of my junior year the Watergate hearings began, and I headed back to Washington and another internship, this time at the Washington bureau of the *New York Times*.

The atmosphere at the *Times* was the exact opposite of NBC the previous summer. Here, the reporters and editors wore elegant clothes and had refined manners. There was very little jocularity, no sexism. The bureau chief was the elderly Clifton Daniel, who was married to Margaret Truman, the former president's daughter. When he walked into the newsroom, a reverent hush descended. Rumor was that he had had the furniture in his office specially made so that it would not wrinkle his suits. James Reston wrote his columns out of a large, comfortable private office, as did William Safire. The reporters wrote their stories on manual typewriters, and as they finished each page they would hold it up and say "copy" just loud enough for one of the copyboys to hear them. It was my first contact with the Eastern establishment, and I did my best to blend in. My clothes were all wrong but a few of the reporters were friendly, or at least polite. Most ignored me.

It was the summer of 1973. Both the *Times* and Congress were relentlessly pursuing Nixon, and I got to work on small pieces of the Watergate story. I was sent to a reporters' breakfast with Mike Mansfield, the Senate majority leader, to listen to his comments about the latest developments at the Senate's hearings, and I got to work on a huge card file detailing every piece of information that had come in about every aspect of the case.

I also got to do some work for Seymour Hersh, the country's leading investigative reporter, who was busy working on exposing details concerning the previously undisclosed bombing of Cambodia. He had me tracking down pilots who had flown the secret missions.

Hersh did not fit the cultural mode of the *Times*. He was rumpled, friendly, sloppily dressed. Several times over that summer I found him after lunch in the men's room with his pants off, trying to pat them down on the counter, because they were wet—he had gotten caught in a thunderstorm and never had an umbrella. The first time I was introduced to him, he was on the phone, and signaled for me to wait. His end of the conversation sounded completely casual, perhaps his wife, I thought, and a discussion of what time he'd get home. And then, at the end: "Thanks, Dr. Kissinger."

When I got hold of some of the pilots and told them I was calling from the *New York Times*, I could hear anguish in their voices, and that shook me. They knew immediately why I was calling—and I realized that protesting college students weren't the only ones suffering at the hands of an out-of-control government. I wanted to talk to them at length, hear their opinions about everything, ask them about their lives, but dutifully handed the phone to Hersh.

I was exactly where I wanted to be. The *Times* Washington newsroom felt like the political nerve center of the universe. It was thrilling, and print journalism seemed like a possible path for me—until I started talking to reporters about what I would need to do when I finished school. Every one of them said the same thing: I would need to spend a minimum of five years at a local or regional newspaper before being considered by the *Times*, in a place like Little Rock or Nashville or Hartford.

No no no,

I wrote in my journal.

I've worked on Watergate and the secret bombing of Cambodia and I need to chase fires in Little Rock, or cover the city council in Nashville??

The arrogance of youth.

* * *

I returned to Ann Arbor for my senior year. I would do honors in political science, of course, and that meant writing a thesis. I chose as my topic "Children and Watergate." The political socialization of children had been a hot topic in political science in the two decades prior, and the dominant theory was that the peace and functionality of American democracy, combined with the psychological need of children to see authority as benevolent, meant that children idealized political leaders, especially the president. Watergate, I thought, presented an opportune test case—the country was, at the moment, neither peaceful nor functional. Did children still idealize the president when he was so clearly a crook who brought the nation to crisis? No, I discovered. How much did they absorb about what was happening? Quite a bit, it turned out. I designed a questionnaire and administered it in several Ann Arbor public school classrooms. I computerized the data, which took forever—this was the age of IBM cards—analyzed it using statistical techniques—no personal computers yet, just central computing centers—and also did follow-up interviews with a subset of the children.

It was absorbing and great fun. Up until senior year I had always studied at the undergraduate library, at a large table, usually in the basement, shared with friends and friends of friends, lots of whispering and quiet laughing, lots of coffee breaks. I still went there to do work for my classes, but now I needed storage space for my computer printouts, and was able to get a small locker at the much larger, more imposing, graduate library, which stood at the very center of campus. It felt like a maze, with an elevator opening on both sides, one side to the ancient, dark original building, the other side to the massive new addition, where the lockers were located.

The whole place felt comfortable to me. Along the outer edges of one of the upper floors, where I worked, were individual carrels with large windows overlooking the campus and town. There was absolute silence. In those carrels I poured over my numbers and wrote my thesis. Hours could go by and I would lose track of time, be late for dinner. Once I forgot it was my turn to cook, and picked up a pizza on my way home for my starving, angry housemates.

That year I was living off campus with a group of friends. NBC, we called it: The No Bullshit Commune. We had the second floor and the attic of a narrow, ramshackle house, and I had my own tiny room at the back of the second floor. In the fall and spring, when the windows were open, in the late afternoon I could hear a choir practicing at a nearby church. I would come home from campus around 4:00, lie on the bed, listen to their voices and doze.

One night when it was again my turn to cook I put LSD in the salad by mistake. A housemate had put a liquid form of the drug onto thin slips of white cardboard and hidden them in the vegetable drawer of the refrigerator; it looked to me like jicama. One of my other housemates, Debra, caught the mistake before we all sat down.

I removed the white slips from the salad.

Debra was a ballet enthusiast, and one gorgeous, warm Saturday evening in October we went to a dance concert. When we got home, my roommates and various friends started shouting, "Harry, Harry, you won't believe what happened."

Nixon had fired Archibald Cox, the Watergate special prosecutor—Cox had issued a subpoena for the White House tapes—recordings Nixon had been making of his conversations with his aides. Nixon ordered the Attorney General to fire Cox. Both the Attorney General and the Deputy Attorney General refused and resigned. Solicitor General Robert Bork did not resign, and did the actual firing.

"What do we do, what do we do?" everyone asked me.

"We send a telegram to the White House," I said, "demanding that Cox be reinstated."

It was the second constitutional crisis of the Nixon administration, after the Pentagon Papers, and a deeper one. Many believed the very structures of constitutional government were crumbling, a historian wrote, without exaggeration, in 2012. I had not yet taken any constitutional law, and thought I had better. I had already applied to graduate school in political science, and was thinking I would study the presidency, or public opinion, perhaps. But in my last semester, I took a course on civil liberties from Milt Heumann, a new, young faculty member finishing his dissertation at Yale. One of the first assignments was to read *West Virginia v. Barnette*, a case from 1943 in which the Supreme Court declared unconstitutional a state law requiring that all schoolchildren salute the flag, including Jehovah's Witnesses, who considered the salute to be worship of a graven image and were unwilling to comply.

The rhetoric in the case is stirring, perhaps the most stirring ever written by the Court—a ringing defense of civil liberties by Justice Robert Jackson for the majority, and a dissent from Justice Frankfurter, stressing the importance of judicial restraint. Frankfurter's dissent begins with an extraordinary personal statement—that he is a Jew, a member of "the most vilified and persecuted minority in history." Yet he must, he says, put his personal feelings and preferences aside. The Court should let the state of West Virginia have its way; that is democracy.

I was transfixed. I was hooked. We read case after case, each one more interesting than the next. Subversive speech. Religious minorities. Searches and seizures. The death penalty. Juvenile rights. In each case an argument asking, at the most basic level, about the nation's fundamental commitments. My Jewish genes kicked in; I was completely at home in this type of text, this type of argument, seeking meaning in words, passing back and forth between principle and concrete case, between deductive and inductive logic, this world of endless implications and consequences. I will study constitutional law in graduate school, not the presidency or public opinion as I had been thinking. I had been leaning toward the University of Chicago but will now shoot for Princeton, renowned in the field.

And seven years later I will publish a psychological biography of Frankfurter, one ambitious Jewish boy in the Ivy League analyzing another.

* * *

Graduation. Just before, there was an oral defense of my thesis in front of a committee of faculty, some of whom I had never met, and I was so nervous I tripped and pulled a tendon in my leg the day before; I was on crutches and hobbled into the oral exam room. In every crisis moment of my life, good or bad, I will in the future somehow manage to do something to a tendon in one of my legs.

The oral goes well. I will graduate *summa cum laude*.

By the day of graduation I am off the crutches. It's a gorgeous spring day in early May, not a cloud in sight. As we line up outside around 11:00 a.m. for the procession, almost everyone is drinking or getting high; the police look on, smiling. Gerald Ford is the speaker—an alum, still Vice President, for a few months at least. As he begins speaking, about thirty graduates rise and storm out, screaming about the military budget. They urge others to join them—"walk out, walk out" they yell—but very few do. Ford does not stop speaking. Except for the shouting protestors, there is silence in the vast indoor arena. It's as if no one is breathing.

A fitting end, I think, and I watch Ford carefully. Did he expect this, I wonder? Is it routine these days, being confronted with angry citizens? Ford did not for a moment change his tempo or acknowledge that anything out of the ordinary was happening, and it struck me that this was the perfect metaphor for what had gone wrong in America: The non-acknowledgment of citizens, contempt for their opinions and for protest of any kind. A refusal even to look, much less to see.

Ford's speech ends; there is tepid applause. There are so many graduates, names are not called. We rise as a group and are blessed by the University president.

Later that day, I walk over to the dorm floor where I was housed as a freshman, peek into the room I lived in, talk to the summer school student living there. Compared to my friends—and me, I wonder?—he looks young and innocent and clean-cut.

It was me in this room only a few years ago, but it feels like decades, and I want to remember that other me, when I was deposited in this room when I was eighteen years old at 8:00 a.m. on a Sunday morning.

I wish the current occupant luck. On the way back across campus I stop at the undergraduate library, linger for a while, walk through the basement level, where I spent so many hours.

I buy one more cup of awful coffee from the vending machine in the coffee room. Summer students are already studying. Just outside the coffee room, I sit on a couch and I look at graffiti under the stairs that, for whatever reason, hasn't been erased or painted over in four years: "Sargent Rock's Maxim: Knowledge is Shit."

No, it isn't, I murmur out loud. Nearby students hear me, look up from their books, stare at me, wonder if I'm a townie, a local lunatic, never in short supply in Ann Arbor. I smile.

I walk back to my house slowly, as slowly as I can, to finish packing.

5

THE IVY LEAGUE FOR BEGINNERS

Fred, another Politics graduate student, African American, funny and hip: *This place is pitiful. You know what we should do to liven things up? Stage a cotillion.*

A cotillion? Fred is slightly tipsy, and everyone sitting around the Graduate College basement bar—aptly named "Debasement"—is skeptical.

Yes, a cotillion. Princeton is full of Southerners. We can each come as a character out of Gone With the Wind. *Who you gonna be, Harry?*

Why, I'll be Miss Scarlett. You have to ask?

Twenty-three and still closeted, I lost my nerve, and went as myself. But some friends always called me Miss Scarlett.

* * *

I am here. I am at Princeton. Incredible,

I wrote in my journal on Saturday, August 31, 1974.

It is truly gorgeous.

After summer at home in Chicago—only it wasn't really home any longer, I had been mostly away for four years and my mother had moved back into the city, into a neighborhood I did not know—my sister Danna and her new, second husband drove me to central New Jersey in their van. I arrived rumpled and exhausted—we'd driven straight through. I was a week early, anxious beyond words to discover what came next.

I wandered around the campus and the town. That first, late summer week, before orientation, before meeting my fellow students or the faculty, I had little to do but to drink in the beauty of the campus, and what sunk in was how completely different it felt from Ann Arbor. This was indeed a different league, not the Midwest, not the Big Ten.

I had arrived on a new continent, apprehensive but determined to conquer.

An Ivy League campus is, above all, graceful, a stark contrast to the utilitarian buildings and sprawl of Ann Arbor and other state universities and towns. There are no jarring vistas, no modern dental school plopped down next to a decrepit old computer center. Money seemed almost to drip from the buildings and landscapes. There were beautiful quadrangles and ancient trees. Old buildings here were lovingly preserved, the architecture often distinguished and—like everything else—understated. The buildings had simple lines and a modest scale.

I stood in front of Nassau Hall, the main administration building. Built in 1754—1754!—occupied by the British during the Revolutionary War, then later, for a brief few months in 1783, the meeting place of the Continental Congress. I walked in, reverent, feeling sheepish that I was wearing shorts. I smelled the old wood and stone. I looked at the winding, narrow staircase, stone steps now worn with age, and wondered what founding father stepped there.

I went back into the quad, stood in front of Whig and Clio, two small buildings with pillars, home to the oldest college literary and debating club in the United States. Aaron Burr had been a member. So were Light-Horse Harry Lee, John Foster Dulles, Adlai Stevenson, and Ralph Nader.

I cannot believe I am where I am. I have studied American history, I know James Madison and Woodrow Wilson walked along these same paths. Madison belonged to the Whigs as a student, Wilson presided over the university from Nassau Hall.

I walk farther and come to a small hill, and across a wide street I see Corwin Hall, a simple red brick building housing the Politics department, with a lovely plaza and fountain in front of it, the Woodrow Wilson School to one side. Corwin was a great constitutional scholar, the greatest of his day, and that is what I am here to study. I stand across the street for a long time. I am not ready to go in, I want to take it slow. I just look.

We do not need to impress, all these buildings say. We know who we are. The simple, occasionally stately architecture, the aura of money, the grace and the understatement are a challenge: *Do you fit in?*

I would. I was sure I would, through sheer force of will if necessary. Scarlett O'Hara had nothing on me.

I want to be special. I want to be liked.

Almost four decades later, my ambition, starkly recorded in my journal, startles and embarrasses me. But I know it was there. I was more than determined. I had placed a huge wager here and I needed it to pay off—all my eggs were in this gilt-edged basket. I would make it work.

And, remarkably, almost miraculously, it did work. Princeton gave me the academic success, and the pedigree, I craved. It gave me so much success, in fact, so fast, so overwhelming, that doubts, hesitations, uncertainties, explorations, slow, steady development, trial and error—the ordinary stuff of early adulthood—were all shoved aside as I raced for academic glory. The Ivy League for me was a speeding train and it was traveling fast, very fast.

I could have gone elsewhere—Harvard, Stanford, Berkeley, the University of Chicago—all accepted me, offered me fellowships. Remember this in later years, Kent Jennings, my undergraduate advisor said to me—"that so many universities wanted you." After the letters of acceptance came from these places, phone calls followed, famous professors, names I knew, courting *me*! My Ann Arbor housemates were as astonished as I. Alan, now a doctor, answered the phone one noontime while we were eating lunch, then casually handed it to me while he ate his cottage cheese—"Berkeley," he said, feigning nonchalance. After I got off the phone, he said, not looking up from the newspaper, "Ho hum, another day, another offer." I felt sheepish. Alan had not yet heard from any medical schools, although soon enough he would.

Princeton did not call (*we know who we are . . . do you fit in?*). But Princeton's course catalogue was an elegant grey, with a simple insignia on the cover, and made their graduate seminars sound wonderful. My best friends from college were headed to Manhattan, an hour away by train, and Princeton had an unmistakable aura—academic gowns were required at dinner in the graduate dining hall, according to the catalogue—though by the time I arrived in September, 1974, that custom had mostly disappeared.

I craved the aura, the way perhaps only a Midwesterner can. The South and the West have their own proud cultures, but the Midwest has always been the country's poor step-child, the provinces, *less than*, and Midwesterners have always cast longing glances eastward, filled with desire. I knew that not all that much time had passed since Princeton had relaxed its Jewish quota, and I knew how intimately connected it had always been to the American establishment, to wealth and power. It was too much to resist.

That first semester, doubts did creep in. Should I have turned down or postponed the fellowship, taken a year off to figure out if this really was the right path? Should I do that now? Was there an alternative to academic life? But as I pondered, no clear picture emerged, so my doubts did not last long. They were swept away as I became absorbed by the material I studied, by the acceptance I felt from my fellow-students and especially my professors, who lavished a degree of attention on me I had never experienced at gigantic Michigan, and found extraordinary. Me? A name I've seen in the *American Political Science Review*, someone reviewed in the *New York Times*, is impressed with *me*? Thinks I'm smart, likes talking to me, wants me to do well, is willing to certify *me* as an intellectual?

Heroin couldn't have given me more of a rush.

The first faculty member with whom I bonded, and a key to my success in graduate school, was a complete surprise: Robert C. Tucker, a Russian specialist, who was not someone I expected to work with. I had studied domestic American politics and I knew nothing important about the USSR, except where to locate it on a map. Big Bob, some graduate students called him, although he was slender, elegant, spoke softly—a thoroughbred, I later called him—and he drank like a fish, as did almost everyone at Princeton.

This aspect of the Ivy League was new to me. Martinis before dinner, wine with dinner, sometimes with lunch. Sherry in the afternoon or before lunch, or late in the evening. Forty years later, as I watched an Oberlin undergraduate go off to the Ivy League, he asked me how he could fit in. "Drink sherry, wear sweaters," I told him.

Bob Tucker, my first role model, did both. He had been an American diplomat in Moscow in the difficult years immediately after World War II, had married a Russian woman and struggled to get her to the United States, and that experience in Stalin's Soviet Union seemed to have left him nervous, anxious, skittish. He had written a well-known book on Karl Marx and was now hard at work on a major biography of Stalin, the first volume of which had just been published and received a great deal of attention, including a laudatory review in the Sunday *New York Times* just before I arrived on campus. When I saw it there one Sunday, a few weeks before leaving my mother's house, I was thrilled.

Bob had concluded that Stalin's personality was the key to some of his otherwise unexplainable behavior, and that brought him deeply into the field of psychology. During my first semester at Princeton I enrolled in his seminar, Personality and Politics. That seminar, along with my interest in the law, gave me direction.

The material in Bob's seminar captivated me. We read Freud, Erik Erikson, Karen Horney. We read theories of leadership. We read biographies. We read *Woodrow Wilson and Colonel House,* a psychological study about Wilson's struggle as president of Princeton with the dean of the graduate school, a struggle focusing on whether there would be a separate graduate quadrangle . . . where I was living.

In Bob's seminar the way I looked at the world shifted. I began to think about unconscious and half-conscious motivation, about why people say what they say, do what they do, seek office and honor. I became a skeptic. I became wary. In a way, this was yet another version of what I already knew about politics—that there was an official story and then there was the real story; it turned out it was true of people as well. I had taken one psychology course in college but it was all stimulus and response, gerbil sleep patterns. This was different, this was real, something I understood. And reading psychological theory helped me understand myself, my family dynamics, in ways I had not thought about. No doubt, that was one of the reasons I was so drawn to it. *Sublimation. Ah, so that's what I've been doing.* I wanted to dig deeper, into other people's personalities and psyches, which I would eventually do in my dissertation, and into myself. I began seeing a therapist on the staff of the Princeton health service, the first in a long line of therapists, some good, some not so good, who helped me peel away my personality one layer at a time. Bob Tucker's seminar began for me what became a long journey.

Beyond the material in his seminar, there was Bob's warmth. On Friday evenings he invited small groups of graduate students to his house after dinner, where he and Evgenia served white wine and we talked about everything from the day's headlines to the latest Princeton gossip, of which there was always an endless supply. I was amazed to be invited to these Friday night gatherings, amazed that a professor was so personally warm, inviting me into his home, not just once but on an ongoing basis. I was the only first year graduate student there, and felt . . . special, that specialness I so desperately craved.

Bob liked my written work, gave me an A+ in the seminar. And, as fate would have it, one of his best friends and his tennis partner was Walter Murphy, the legal scholar in the department, so that when I enrolled in Murphy's seminar the following semester, he had already heard about me from Bob, and was predisposed to think well of me.

The lives and careers of graduate students turn on such things. Bob Tucker and Walter Murphy played tennis together, nearly every day . . . the purest chance. In later years I would wonder: Where would I be now if things had been slightly different that first year as Princeton? Where would I be if Bob and Walter had had a falling out and no longer played tennis, or if one of them had been away on sabbatical that year, or if I had written one bad paper for Bob? What if I hadn't taken Bob's seminar?

But I did take it, and the next semester, Bob taught an undergraduate course on leadership, and asked me to be a preceptor for the course—what Princeton calls a teaching fellow—and this too was special, since first year students were usually not allowed to teach.

This was his greatest gift. I loved the classroom immediately. I found I had an ability to ask good questions, to enliven the material, to push just hard enough so that the students could see what they needed to see, and they responded . . . and seemed to like me. When the discussions were lively I felt wonderful, found it thrilling to engage in the give and take. The undergraduates sometimes invited me to their eating clubs for a meal, took me out for beer, came to my office hours and, sometimes, told me their troubles. And by the middle of the semester, Bob occasionally called me for advice about the course and even asked me to deliver one lecture, which I did—happily.

I don't think I ever worked so hard as I did writing that first lecture; it took me the better part of two weeks. Standing at the lectern, feeling like I was getting something across, was a new sensation. On some level, teaching, when it goes well, gives the teacher a feeling of agency, of personal power: I have the ability to boil this down, get it across, enter the minds of the people listening, make them think, make them see. My version of reality is entering their psyches, if only for a moment. I liked the feeling—it can be intoxicating—and the lecture was a success. The students even clapped when I finished. At the beginning of the next class, Bob began by saying "Mr. Hirsch was so good I was afraid he might put me out of business."

Several of my fellow graduate students came to hear the lecture, and one of the unusual things about Princeton's graduate program was the degree to which graduate students spent time together outside of class. This was in large part a function of the fact that Princeton is a small, very expensive town. Single graduate students had few options other than living in the Graduate College. This meant we took meals together and socialized, and I learned a great deal over dinner and made some very good friends that way. Although we couldn't have said so at the time, this was also good preparation for becoming a faculty colleague. We learned how to talk about our discipline and our particular subjects in meaningful ways, how to defend ourselves from criticism, how to take an interest in someone else's work. I was astonished, later, when serving as a faculty member at other places, to hear how isolated most graduate students felt. At Princeton I felt just the opposite.

But it had been a long journey from Ann Arbor to Princeton, far more than 614 miles—at least it was then, for me. My fellow students, the people I had been getting to know, had gone to Wellesley, Colgate, Williams, and I saw that Midwestern openness was not quite the right style. So I started holding my knife and fork differently, in the Ivy/British manner, fork in the right, knife in the left, no shifting the fork from one hand to the other. I wore more khaki and button-down oxford shirts, the uniform. Shoes without socks in warmer weather. I read biographies and novels about Princeton and Princetonians, F. Scott Fitzgerald, Woodrow Wilson. I did not feel that I quite belonged there, and I wondered, sometimes, what I was doing, especially after a dismal January of writing long papers on a deserted campus in the middle of several blizzards.

* * *

April. Spring. Second semester of my first graduate year. I have two seminars on Thursday, one in the afternoon I no longer remember, and one in the evening with Walter Murphy, Comparative Constitutional

Law. Murphy is McCormick Professor of Jurisprudence, the chair occupied in every generation by perhaps the country's leading constitutional scholar, beginning with Woodrow Wilson himself. I want to impress him, and am nervous about my every comment, every intervention in class discussions.

We have a moot court. I am assigned to play one of the attorneys, and I have to present an oral argument. I do not remember what the case was about, nor what I said. The weather was suddenly warm and muggy and there was a thunderstorm, I was drenched. My mind has never been sharp after dinner, and especially after a long afternoon seminar, it takes effort to focus. I am so tired, wet, and miserable that I must run on pure adrenaline, making most of it up as I go along. At times I can push myself this way, force myself to perform when there is no energy, and tonight is one of those times.

I sit down after my presentation, and Joan Tronto (still a friend and colleague, forty years later) whispers "you were superb, Harry." I am startled . . . I was just trying to get through it. The next day Walter Murphy sends around to the whole department, faculty and graduate students, some sort of announcement about a pending department policy, and humorously says that if anyone has comments he "will send my learned counsel Harry Hirsch to discuss the matter."

Murphy becomes my advisor, and his word gets me an appointment at Harvard. Years later, I think: Everything followed from that wet Thursday night.

* * *

The moot court, teaching, my lecture, seminars: Never in my life, before or since, did things fall so seamlessly into place as they did that first academic year at Princeton. Scarlett confronted Ashley with her love while the other maidens at the Twelve Oaks Bar-b-q were asleep upstairs in the afternoon, and Ashley swept her into his arms and kissed her passionately. They soon married, and Melanie became aunt to their many children. The boys grew strong and handsome and went to Princeton, as many Southern gentlemen did. Lincoln let the South leave the Union peacefully, there was no war, Scarlett never had to marry men she didn't love or sell lumber in Atlanta just to survive.

Ah, but then Scarlett wouldn't be Scarlett, would she, and the novel would have remained an obscure Southern romance. Scarlett started so well, was so gifted as a flirt, who could imagine the hardship that was coming, that her mother would die and her father go mad, that Scarlett would have to deliver Melanie and Ashley's baby as Sherman marched through Georgia, burning everything in sight? How could any of that possibly happen? Scarlett was dancing, and the music was sweet.

The summer after my first year the music stopped, just for a moment. Scarlett's feet hurt, and she worried; yes, all the men chase me, but who will marry me and what is my future? Do I *really* want to stay in Georgia and live on a plantation for the rest of my life? What happens when I'm no longer the sweet young thing?

No, I wasn't sure the academic life was for me after all, no matter how well I seemed to be doing. For something beckoned a mere hour away by train: Manhattan. My good friends and housemates from college—Deb, Edie, Alan—were there, Alan in medical school, Deb and Edie living incredibly exciting lives in the west Seventies, where cheap apartments could be had and the streets were unimaginably alive. I would visit them, sleep on their floors, and we would explore the city. Deb tried to become a dance critic, and we would walk to Lincoln Center and see the New York City Ballet for a few dollars. Edie loved opera, and somehow procured cheap tickets to the opening of the Met in October. We mingled with the glitterati (coloratura Roberta Peters, in the audience, accidentally stepped on my toe at intermission), and then on New Year's Eve got very dressed up and went to see *La Boheme*. Standing room cost little, and after an act or two the rich New Yorkers in gowns and tuxedoes with orchestra seats would give their stubs to those of us standing in the back.

And, most tempting of all: Manhattan's gay life was exploding, beckoning, was on display everywhere during that brief honeymoon between Stonewall and the first AIDS cases, a mere dozen years. What am I doing in bucolic, dull, straight Princeton, studying all the time, I would think. I belong there, in the city. Isn't *that* the ball I want to attend? What am I doing at Twelve Oaks, at Tara, lovely though they may be?

The crisis hit full force in the summer after my first year, when I stayed in Princeton and briefly shared a house with a few other graduate students. It was not a good summer. I didn't like the house, had to take a dull language class every morning to pass my French language exam, and did boring research work for Fred Greenstein in an airless office. Fred was an absolute sweetheart, like Bob an expert on personality and politics, whose work on children and politics had been crucial to my undergraduate thesis. I needed the money but the work was mind-numbing—recording titles for a computerized bibliography on the presidency—and I thought about leaving Princeton, going to New York, getting a job, living like my friends, and, um, finally coming completely out of the closet.

I confided in Edie about my dilemma. Edie, like me, had thought she wanted to be an academic, entered the graduate program in Romance Languages at Yale, but dropped out, went to New York, was working for a talent agent, and had a wonderful first floor apartment on West 74th Street. "You need a break," Edie said to me, and she hit a nerve. Why *did* I rush immediately into graduate school? Didn't I need time just to live? What if I went to law school in a little while; then couldn't I choose to stay in Manhattan? Meanwhile, couldn't I have a *life?*

So in mid-July I looked in the *Times* classifieds and found a minor magazine looking for advertising staff. I was offered the job, and even looked at a studio apartment on West 81st Street renting for $200/month. (I checked recently, just for fun; both Edie's apartment on 74th and the apartment I almost rented on 81st St. are now floors of renovated townhouses. One of them recently sold for $18 million.)

Back in Princeton I confided in my friend Gail Russell that I was thinking of leaving. "Oh but Harry, you have so much to give," Gail said when we talked about a future of teaching, and that hit a nerve as well. I confided in my friend Chuck Beitz, who understood my impulse to leave but counseled caution. He pointed out how well I was doing, that I might actually get a teaching job at a place I wanted to be, not in Nebraska (that was our standard running joke—a temporary teaching job at a bible college in Nebraska).

I gave in. I decided to stay, at least for another year, take my general exams, get the Master's degree that would come when I passed them. I would decide later about a dissertation and a PhD, or whether to go to law school. I'll think about that tomorrow, Scarlett said.

So the music stopped, but only for a moment. By the beginning of my second year I was back at the ball, and this time the music went on for quite a while. I did well in my second-year seminars, and again did well as a preceptor, this time for Walter Murphy's course, Constitutional Interpretation. Murphy began the first lecture in that course by saying "this course has a reputation as the hardest in the College . . . if it's true, it's by design, not by accident." He gave only one lecture per week, and the preceptors met with students for two hours, not one, as in other courses.

I loved teaching those two-hour seminars. Constitutional law was the perfect subject to generate especially animated discussion. It was easy to spark lively give and take, or so it seemed so to me. Con law cases provide the perfect blend, for teaching, of concrete facts and abstract principle, and there are almost always good arguments on each side of a case.

Once again I did very well, and loved what I was doing. I was surprised and excited to discover that teaching was about relating—relating to the kids and using that relationship to guide them to and through the material. I found that I intuitively understood where they stood, what they knew, what they didn't know, what they wanted and needed to know. I seemed to have a knack for asking the right question at the right moment, a question that would advance the discussion and make it come more alive. My instincts were usually on target—not 100 percent of the time, but often enough. And I enjoyed, especially, when I was able to make the discussion flow, when I could get them arguing with each other without much intervention, and when I was able to push a student to reconsider her position. If they pushed in one direction, I pushed in the other. I was having fun.

Murphy good-naturedly complained that my teaching evaluations were higher than his; I quickly developed a reputation as a very good teacher, and being a good undergraduate teacher was important at Princeton. I was dancing still, and this particular music—the music of teaching—was my favorite.

As I think back, I see myself in the classroom, usually a windowless room deep in the bowels of the Woodrow Wilson School building, and then, before and after seminars and undergraduate classes, I see myself lying on my bed in the Graduate College for hours on end, reading, always reading, reading so much that soon I needed a stronger prescription in my glasses, which I could hardly afford. I remember that I was so absorbed reading Ronald Dworkin's *Taking Rights Seriously*, which had just been published, that I lost track of time and missed dinner, and so impressed by Roberto Unger's *Law In Modern Society*—a mess of a book, but brilliant—that I said no when friends wanted to go to the Princeton Diner, out on the highway away from campus, as we sometimes did around ten or eleven at night. And when I read Freud for Bob Tucker's seminar, I stayed up until 3:00 a.m. several nights in a row, and one night did not sleep at all.

As Jimmy Carter wracked up delegate votes, I took my general exams in May of my second year, as required, and began working on a dissertation just two days later, probably to keep myself from thinking too much about moving to Manhattan, where what waited for me was . . . what, exactly? Princeton was paying my way through graduate school, full fellowship and living stipend, but I knew enough to know that Columbia or NYU, or any other law school, would not do the same. That would have meant massive debt to get a law degree, which, I also knew, would restrict my choice of job when I finished. And even in 1976 one could see that a real life in New York—not a weekend, but a real life—required money. As attractive as it might be at the moment, one could live la vie boheme in a tiny dilapidated walk-up apartment for only so long. That opera ended in disease and death, after all.

So I plunged ahead at Princeton, and was determined to get through a dissertation quickly; I didn't want to pause and let doubts creep in.

Many years later, I realized, with a chill running down my spine, that that decision, to stay in graduate school and finish, undoubtedly saved my life. If I had paused for a while or chosen a different path, I would have joined my friends in New York, and these were the pre-plague years, when nobody knew what was coming.

Staying in Princeton, I wanted to find a dissertation topic that would combine my interest in psychology and leadership with my interest in the Supreme Court and constitutional law, and there was an obvious choice: a biography of a Supreme Court Justice. Scholars in my field had written any number of such judicial biographies, it was a staple of the field—at least up to that point—and I could apply the psychological tools I had learned from Bob Tucker and Fred Greenstein. All I needed was a subject.

I had one. As an undergraduate I had noticed in Felix Frankfurter's written opinions a kind of fussiness, a tendency to overwrite, a brand of stubbornness. I began gathering materials about him, and became more and more intrigued. I sensed there was a story, a personal story, about him, into which no one had yet really looked, a story that had a profound influence on the jurist he would become. And I discovered that although there were a few biographies written about him, none were more than superficial. His life story was fascinating, and represented something I knew, knew well, knew in my bones, for I was living it: the Jewish-American immigrant experience—the deep desire to be let *in*. Then I found out that most of Frankfurter's Court papers at Harvard had only recently been opened to scholars, and that his personal letters were at the Library of Congress, a short train ride away from Princeton. I was off and running.

Running is the word. By August—only three months after passing my general exams—Walter Murphy mentions casually when he passes me in the hallway of Corwin Hall that he needed a copy of my CV—my résumé—because there was a job available at Ohio State.

I didn't have a CV, so I went back to my room and typed one up. Two months later, standing in the department office, Murphy tells me, casual as can be, that there is also a job at Harvard. Was I interested? He's holding a letter in his hands and I can see the Harvard letterhead.

Did Scarlett want to go to the grandest ball of the decade?

I was twenty-four years old. I had been in graduate school for two years; the average time to degree was five or six years. Many took longer, and some did post-docs after receiving the PhD. I had found a good dissertation topic, done some preliminary work on it, hoped that it would eventually come together—I was finding rich material in Frankfurter's letters to his future wife, which most scholars had overlooked—but had only scratched the surface. I was at the beginning, not even the middle, of the work. I had notes, just notes. No pages, no chapters, no manuscript.

But when you are a desperately ambitious twenty-four-year-old and your advisor dangles a job at Harvard, you do not ask questions. You do not pause and think. You lunge. You go back to your room in the Graduate College and type up a CV. Miss Scarlett knew in her bones that this was a once-in-a-lifetime chance. She was not about to let it slip away, or hesitate over little matters like finishing some work or not being quite ready.

Later, when I worked with my own graduate students, I saw how long it took even very good ones to shape a dissertation and get the damned thing finished, and I would wonder: what in the world was

Walter Murphy thinking, sending me out on the job market so soon? Did he have so much confidence in me that he just knew I would write a good dissertation? If so, he was taking quite a gamble with my career—lots of terrifically smart graduate students flame out over a dissertation. Or did he not think it through? He got a letter, he opened it, I was standing there . . . he mentions it, because it seemed it might apply to me. Or perhaps was the temptation of sending a student to Harvard too great to resist? After all, part of one's reputation as a scholar is the ability to place graduate students in good jobs.

I never found out, never had the courage to ask him what he had been thinking before he died, and at the time, I wasn't asking questions. If it had been Fred Greenstein or Bob Tucker, they might have asked, "Do you feel ready, do you think this is the right time?" But my relationship with Murphy was different, more formal. He was always "Professor Murphy," not "Fred" or "Bob." Murphy, born in Charleston and a practicing Catholic, had served with the marines in Korea, been decorated with the Distinguished Service Cross, and retained a fairly strong conservative air (and haircut). One didn't over-analyze the task at hand, one didn't dawdle. One did the work, did whatever needed to be done, and got on with it.

Working with an advisor with such a persona had its advantages. Getting on with it is not a bad strategy for getting through graduate school, where so many linger and drift and fall away, especially at the dissertation stage. But also, I now see, I was a bit afraid of Murphy— afraid to give him any unpolished or sloppy work, which was a good thing, certainly, but also afraid to ask too many questions, which was not. Talking things through—processing—was not his style, and neither was advice. Marines don't process, and they don't give advice.

Murphy was a genuine eccentric, and after I left graduate school neither the eccentricity nor the formality of our relationship ever entirely went away. There were always problems when we tried to connect. There was the time we were to have dinner in Washington, but he gave me the name of the wrong restaurant, and then a similar experience about a lunch in Boston. We appeared together at the APSA on a panel about my second book, and he said he would send me the notes for his critique in advance, but sent them to the wrong address, so I was blindsided by his remarks, which were harsh. We were scheduled to appear on another panel together at another conference and then to have lunch, but he never showed up.

Then there was the desk. Through a friend of his, a Princeton elder, Murphy had acquired a handsome writing desk that had once belonged to Felix Frankfurter. The elder had been a law clerk to William O. Douglas, who had served on the Court with Frankfurter, and somehow the desk wound up in his possession. The elder left it to Murphy, and Murphy said he would leave it to me.

By the time he was ready to pass it along to me, we had not seen or spoken to each other in many years. So, after a long silence and a public dust-up over the question of gay rights, he sent me a curt email, offering me the desk, so long as I paid the freight from Albuquerque, where he was then living in retirement. No greeting, no hello, no "hope you are well," no chit chat, just a transaction about a piece of furniture.

But all that was far in the future when he sent me out on the job market.

In October I flew to Columbus and then was offered the Ohio State job within a few days, which astonished everyone. I promptly turned it down. My fellow-graduate students, and most of the faculty, were aghast—*you're turning down a tenure-track job at a major university?*—but Miss Scarlett was not about to settle for one of the Tarleton twins. No, Miss Scarlett had her eye on the main chance, and knew it when it came a-courtin.

So in December, my friend Louise Haberman helped me choose my interview clothes for Harvard—blue blazer, grey flannel slacks, black loafers, red and blue striped tie. Not a suit; "too obvious," Louise said, "go for *understated*" (Louise had gone to Cornell). I asked her if it would be ok to wear a hat, and we debated what kind. No ski cap, certainly, no hood on a parka. "Something conservative," Louise said, "close to a fedora." "But my ears will be cold," I complained. "First impressions," she reminded me, "are everything."

I flew up to Boston in my new hat in a blizzard in early January. My first one-on-one interview at 9:00 a.m. was with Harvey Mansfield, chair of the department and a conservative icon. We sat opposite each other in two plush leather armchairs in his office. The chairman was wearing a blue blazer, grey flannel slacks, black loafers, and a striped tie.

It felt like a scene in a movie, though not one I had ever been in. I relaxed. Perhaps I would fit in here, I thought.

The night before, John Jackson, a member of the search committee, had hosted a dinner at his home in Belmont, a town next to Cambridge full of old, graceful houses. I walked into his living room, was introduced to some faculty and faculty spouses, and stood in front of the fire (my toes were frozen; the loafers didn't provide much warmth in the snow). James Q. Wilson greeted me and asked me how his old friend Walter Murphy was doing—it turned out they had been in graduate school together. We chatted casually about Jimmy Carter, about to be inaugurated, and about "Pat" Moynihan, who was leaving Cambridge because he had just been elected to the Senate from New York.

Of course. A colleague can be elected to the United States Senate. Nothing special.

So this is how it works, I thought to myself. Walter plays tennis with Bob Tucker and went to graduate school with Jim Wilson. Harvard hires from Princeton and Princeton hires from Harvard. You go to the right school and work with the right people (and do good work, certainly) and there you are, holding a glass of sherry in front of the fire, casually chatting about a colleague just elected to the Senate with one of the most famous political scholars of the twentieth century, probably the world's leading expert on crime.

Miss Scarlett knew that underneath the casual banter at the dinner, behind the smiles and low-key chat, she was being examined, inspected, looked over carefully—could she chat amiably? Did she have good table manners? *We know who we are, do you fit in?* But this did not make her nervous. This was, after all, what she wanted, what she had come East to get, and she knew that even to have gotten this far—to be standing in this living room in Belmont, in front of the fire—represented something, was an achievement.

The next day there were a series of one-on-one meetings with faculty, and the main event, a presentation on my dissertation over bag lunches at High Noon. One by one the famous names walked in and were introduced to me, and I shook their famous hands. Sid Verba. Michael Walzer. Sam Beer. Judith Shklar. They ate their lunches while I spoke, then asked me questions while most of them smoked (this was 1977). Some of the questions were tough, some slightly hostile—why are you examining Frankfurter's psyche instead of his ideas?—but I answered calmly ("actually, I'm examining the relation between the two") and my answers seemed to go down smoothly. There were nods.

The only moment I was truly nervous that day was meeting one-on-one with Sam Beer. He was chair of the search committee and had actually known Frankfurter. He was an elegant man with British manners (he studied British politics and had advised American presidents) and had an air of complete, if casual, authority. By this time in his career, he was one of Harvard's grand old men. All it would take, I knew, was his saying no, I was wrong about Frankfurter, and that would end my chances. But, miraculously, he thought I was onto something by looking at Frankfurter's personality.

What is astounding to me, as I look back, is how confident I felt during most of the interview. I was young, very young, and talking about a dissertation not a page of which had actually been written. I had worked on the research for barely six months . . . yet there I was, presenting it to the Harvard Government department.

Miss Scarlett knew when it was time to perform, when everything was on the line. She sparkled.

And the grandees of Atlanta seemed to like it, accept it. Six weeks later, the invitation came. It took them a while to make up their minds, of course, and in the weeks of waiting there was another interview at a very good place—the University of Washington in Seattle—and then one Tuesday while working in the Frankfurter papers at the Library of Congress, one of the librarians left a note at my table while I was at lunch. "Call Professor Mansfield at Harvard." I knew the faculty had met the night before—they always met on the first Monday evening of the month—and so I had left word where I could be found and knew a decision would come that Tuesday. No word had come in the morning, and I started to worry.

For lunch, instead of the library cafeteria, to calm my nerves I walked over to the Supreme Court building, and standing in line at their more elegant cafeteria—a line that moved slowly, very slowly, like the Court itself—I stared at the portrait of Justice Brandeis on the wall as I inched my way forward. Brandeis, the first Jew on the Court and one of Frankfurter's mentors, figured prominently in my dissertation. I had been reading his letters (horrible handwriting that nearly drove me insane; I had to use a magnifying glass to decipher many of the words). Would there be a line that connected Brandeis to Frankfurter to me, a line passing through Harvard Yard (Brandeis had been the highest-scoring student ever at the Harvard Law School)? Everything seemed to have meaning that day, especially the look in Brandeis's eyes—wise, a bit playful, a bit sad . . . but above all, wise. I couldn't stop looking at his eyes.

Help me, Louie, I muttered out loud. The woman in front of me turned around and stared at me with an alarmed look on her face. I smiled.

I found the note after lunch, went out to the payphone in the hall to call Cambridge. The job was offered. The chairman apologized for the delay in reaching a decision, saying "we've come to our senses." He was casually disorganized in going over the details. Casual disorganization, I would learn, was a key part of the Harvard style.

That evening I was in a daze. I went back to the Freemans' house—Christy Freeman was a good friend in college, her parents lived in D.C., and they were kind enough to let me stay with them while I worked at the Library of Congress. Mrs. Freeman was away, and Mr. Freeman was working late, so I sat alone, staring at the walls, as I often did when something major occurred in my life, good or bad. Around ten I called Walter Murphy and gave him the news; he was a night owl and I knew he ate dinner at nine. That telephone call is the only time I ever heard any kind of emotion from him.

The excitement hit me the next morning. I was so excited, in fact, I couldn't go back to the library. I took the day off, wandered around the National Gallery and then Georgetown, buying myself a fancy lunch I couldn't afford. I called a few close friends: "So, when are you coming to Cambridge?"

I went back to work. This is serious, I thought to myself. I have to finish this thing. Fast.

A few weeks later, back in Princeton, Nick Wahl, a dapper man I hardly knew who taught French politics, congratulated me and said, "My God, an offer from Harvard without a dissertation. We've been dining out on this for weeks." Many congratulated me, but some of my fellow-students did not, and I discovered something new—academic jealousy. "Well, I guess Walter Murphy can get anyone a job anywhere," one of my fellow students said within earshot at a party. It was meant to be funny but it was also meant to be mean.

Ah, I see. Not everyone is as kind and good as Miss Mellie. Miss Scarlett saw, for the first time, that success had a price.

But most were happy for me. The faculty was thrilled, and I threw myself into the dissertation, which now had a deadline. I had one year.

The job was offered in February, and in June I decided it made sense to move up to Boston, even though I would not start teaching until the following February. The materials I needed for the last part of my dissertation research were at Harvard, I would have had to spend a lot of time there anyway, so why not move? I had done Princeton. Time to move on. I was eager to stop being a graduate student, to become something else, to interact with new friends and colleagues . . . to find my place.

On July 1, I rented a car—afraid to consign my dissertation notes to the movers, who took everything else—and drove to Boston with my friend Marion Smiley; I had hired her to type my dissertation on IBM cards—an early and disastrous word-processing system. The cards were constantly getting mixed up, garbling the text.

I quickly moved into the cheap summer sublet I had found, and that night we went to see a play about Emma Goldman written by the radical historian Howard Zinn.

I never forgot that play. Scenes from it would show up in my dreams, even ten years later. There's a crucial scene where young Emma, sewing in a New York sweatshop, demands that the fire escape door be opened, and speaks up, makes a fuss until the owner opens it. She is realizing her power, the power of a demand, the power of collective action. "I'm opening your door," the owner finally says, repeating it as the stage darkens and the scene ends.

The door was open.

6

THE IVY LEAGUE: ADVANCED

Almost unconsciously, excellence bullies.
— George Steiner

1977, summer, Cambridge. I am desperately trying to finish my dissertation. I have only until February, when I will start teaching. Since my appointment has not yet started, they do not have a real office for me. They give me an office in a small, dilapidated wooden building, a faraway barracks, literally left over from World War II. During the summer no one is around except an unfriendly graduate student in chemistry. Strange smells fill the air, and I am frightened that the graduate student will burn down the barracks and my dissertation with it. I make many copies.

I am living on Beacon Hill in Boston, across the river, at first in a tiny sublet studio. No one can understand why I don't live in Cambridge, but after three years in proper Princeton I know I need space, distance. When I walk around Beacon Hill I feel at home, and this is 1977, there are still cheap apartments to be had. The studio was in a building that overlooked the Charles, but my place was at the back, overlooking an alley. There was no TV (so no movies), not much furniture. There was a stereo and a record collection, though, and the records were wonderful—Ella Fitzgerald, Sarah Vaughn, Keith Jarrett, the jazz pianist, whom I had never heard. I play the records over and over as I try to get to sleep, sentences from what I had written that morning racing through my head.

Every morning, six, sometimes seven days a week, I get up at 5:30, take the Red Line to Harvard Square, and walk to the barracks. There is a manual typewriter in the office, left over from God knows when or who. I like the feel of the keyboard, am tickled by the idea that the typewriter might have been used once to bang out war requisitions, or used by Henry Kissinger or one of his graduate students, rumored to have once had an office in the building when he was a lowly faculty member.

I am at the typewriter by 7:00. I do not know where the words come from—fear, ambition, true knowledge?—but they do come, they pour out of me day after day. I write until noon, when I walk out to the street and buy a sandwich and a bottle of iced tea from a lunch truck. The barracks is so far from Harvard Square I can't spare the time to walk back and forth to have lunch in a real restaurant. After lunch I read over what I have written, correct the text, revise, add the footnotes. I go home on the Red Line and collapse. The routine continues into the fall, which they have given me off to finish the dissertation. For weeks on end I speak to no one.

After a few months I move into a somewhat larger apartment, but it's being renovated, and before I can move in I have to get out of the sublet for two nights. I'm still subsisting on a graduate student stipend, my Harvard salary won't start until the first of the year; I cannot possibly afford a hotel, and I haven't yet met anyone I might be able to stay with. So I spend the two nights on the floor of my office, brush my teeth in the bathroom, take a shower at the Harvard gym, where I persuade the guard to let me in, since I don't yet have an ID card. He takes pity on me and let me shower.

I finish the dissertation, defend it in April. On my twenty-sixth birthday, I teach a graduate seminar in the afternoon (most of the students at least as old, if not older than I), then take the train to New York and the connecting train to Princeton, arriving near midnight. The next day is the public defense, which is unusually crowded. First and second year graduate students, people I do not know, come to watch, some to listen, some to judge, to see who is this guy who landed a job at Harvard. The day of the defense there is an undergraduate demonstration going on, South Africa, and there are rumors that some undergraduates will invade my defense and take over the building, but that does not materialize.

It is a ritual, a dissertation defense, one of those exercises where everyone knows nothing is really at stake, but still I am nervous . . . I am being watched. I get through it, and then there are drinks at Walter Murphy's house, drinks and hearty handshakes. I don't usually drink, haven't since college, but that evening I do—how often do you earn a PhD?—and I am a bit lightheaded as we talk. Everyone wants to know about Harvard, and I do not know what to say. "It's not much like Princeton," I blurt out, finally. "You should be tougher on us, prepare us for what comes next."

My words surprise me, and everyone else. For alas, Miss Scarlett was finding that Atlanta was a much larger and considerably tougher place than Tara and its surroundings. At first she was ignored, and that was bewildering. She was expecting Harvard to be Princeton writ larger. Harvard was something else entirely.

Princeton, both the town and the campus, were small—very small—in comparison to Cambridge, and smallness bred friendliness. That friendliness could sometimes be cloying, but I didn't stay long enough to experience much of that. Every member of the Politics department faculty at Princeton, even those way beyond my field of interest, was at least somewhat friendly, knew who I was, knew and seemed to care about what I was doing. The graduate students socialized together—there wasn't much alternative—and often socialized with the faculty. Along with evenings at Bob Tucker's house, a few grad students played poker with Amy Gutmann, then an assistant professor (now president of the University of Pennsylvania) and Harry Eckstein, one of the most senior members of the faculty. There were parties large and small. Those of us living at the Graduate College often had faculty members to dinner. Princeton was a true community, or at least seemed so to me, and rank didn't seem to matter a whole lot.

No one in Cambridge seemed to realize I was there, much less care, and I doubt anyone in its history ever thought of Harvard's Government department as a community. Rank not only mattered, but mattered a great deal. In fact, it overwhelmed every other consideration.

This was perhaps a remnant of Harvard's Puritan past, I later thought. Either you were a member of the elect—saved—bound for heaven—senior faculty—or you were not. If you were not, members of the elect needn't pay much attention to you . . . and most didn't. They might try to help you a bit on your way, or pity you, but they would never dream of pretending you were anything like an equal. No Friday night wine. Not much socializing at all. No parties. No poker.

Miss Scarlett would have to make her own way.

I did what I could. Early on I ran into Judith Shklar at a bookstore, and, heart pounding, asked her if she would like to have lunch. She said, yes, that was a good idea: "We'll have a good long chat." To chat seemed to be a favorite Harvard verb.

We met at the faculty club—old wood, oriental carpets, shabby-chic—and she used the lunch to tell me about my new colleagues. She went through the list of them alphabetically, in fact, and rapidly—every conversation with Dita (as she was called) was rapid—and with complete nonchalance told me each one's foibles and strengths, both personal and professional—which ones drank, which ones cheated on their wives, which ones had stopped publishing, which ones were truly brilliant. "X is mad," she said about one; "completely demented," she said about another. One was "an idiot ... a mistake," meaning he should never have been appointed. "A really smart boy," she said about one or two of the junior faculty, and it was clear from her tone that this mattered more than anything. Well, I was smart, or so they thought at Princeton. I didn't drink and would never have a wife. So far so good.

What's most interesting about that phrase—"a really smart boy," as I think about it more than thirty years later, is the use of the word "boy." That's what junior faculty were at Harvard—the children. At Princeton, not just junior faculty but graduate students were treated, more or less, as peers, or as peers-in-training, members or potential members of the guild. Harvard was different. It was a shock.

Dita continued through the list in her usual rocket-fire manner. I tried to absorb what I was hearing, but this was not what I expected over my first lunch at the Harvard faculty club. It's hard for me to imagine what kind of look I had on my face as I listened ... I had never heard such a litany. How, exactly, was one supposed to react when one learned that a quite famous senior colleague was a philanderer, or that another drank to excess? I was at a complete loss.

Dita finally noticed the look on my face and paused, briefly. "None of us are here because we're good or nice people," she said with a shrug. I smiled.

Lunch with Dita became a regular occurrence during my years in Cambridge, and I learned enormous amounts from her. After that first lunch, to my relief, we stayed mostly away from dissecting the faculty (although we talked about graduate students endlessly).

Dita was the most brilliant mind I have ever seen up close. Born in Latvia to prosperous Jewish parents, classically educated, with a high-pitched voice like Julia Child, she was a refugee as a young girl from the fast-approaching Nazis, and understood in her bones that politics was no joke. A staunch liberal, she had written books on Rousseau, on Hegel, on utopianism, and a book on legalism, an interest we shared, and she maintained, throughout her work, the single clearest idea about politics I have ever encountered. Politics, she said, is always about the weak and the strong.

Dita befriended me, mentored me, a bit, bullied me, a bit, and lunches and the occasional dinner with her became a sort of post-graduate seminar. The brilliance fell from her like a wild river during a huge storm, overflowing its banks and flooding every nearby town. As I got to know her, I saw that complete frankness about everything—absolutely everything—was an aspect of her formidable intellect. She got to the heart of things, quickly—on occasion, too quickly—whether it was sizing up a colleague (including me) or analyzing Hegel. She told the truth, as she saw it. Take it or leave it. She did not suffer fools. She did not waste time. She did not censor herself.

The other senior colleague I got to know well was Sid Verba, who became chair of the department as soon as I arrived—a lucky break. Sid was an expert on public opinion and probably the world's leading expert on political participation, and we had a connection through Princeton. He had been a graduate student and assistant professor there—Walter Murphy's house in Princeton used to be the Verbas' house—so yet again, I saw how important personal connections could be. Sid was as warm and personable as most were cool and distant. Fairly soon after I arrived, and many times after, he invited me to his house for dinner, which was incredibly kind of him, especially considering that it was not the norm.

At the first dinner with the Verbas at their huge Victorian house in Brookline, the talk was convivial and the atmosphere relaxed, and everyone stayed until well after eleven. There was much laughter. The conversation at one point turned to the Supreme Court—school segregation, affirmative action—and all eyes turned to me. It felt a bit like the job interview redux, but I seemed to pass muster.

Soon after the first dinner at the Verbas came my first department meeting. Drinks at the faculty club at 5:30, general business at 6:00, then dinner. Very civilized, I thought, until a colleague pointed out that the reason it was done that way was that the senior faculty had difficulty conducting business without alcohol smoothing away animosities. After dinner, junior faculty members were expected to quietly leave the table. The senior faculty would remain to talk about the only thing that really mattered, senior appointments.

I was quite nervous on the day of the first department meeting, and the nervousness expressed itself, as it often did in those days—as it had before the Harvard interview—as worry about appearance. What was I supposed to wear? Corduroy jacket, or was that too much of a cliché? Instead of thinking, as I should have, "what in God's name am I doing going to a Harvard faculty meeting at the age of twenty-five," I worried about my clothes.

I settled on my interview blazer—navy blue, how could anyone object—and showed up much too early, but all seemed to go well. I was properly dressed.

The meeting itself went fine, and somehow I got through it without showing my nerves. Everyone chatted during the cocktail hour, and when the meeting started, Sid, chairing, introduced me. At dinner Jim Wilson wondered if his son, approaching college age, should go to Princeton; what was my opinion of it for undergraduates? Leaving with the other juniors at the end of the meal felt strange, and I half expected Dita or Sid to say they would come and tuck us in after our baths.

Apart from Dita and Sid, the people I got to know best were some of my junior colleagues, and those relationships could be wonderful, but also fraught. Harvard does not have a tenure-track system, which means the norm is to spend a period of time there untenured, then move on to another university—but on very rare occasions (at least at the time) an assistant professor would be the exception and earn tenure from within.

This was not a recipe for junior faculty collegiality, especially among junior colleagues in the same subfield. And the senior faculty made matters much worse by playing a pernicious game. Some of them would pull junior colleagues aside, one by one, and whisper, "you know, if you do X, Y, and Z, you might be *the one.*"

Several senior colleagues played the game with me. They would let slip a comment along these lines casually, before or after a department meeting or passing in the hall. One made it a point to come to my office to talk about it. The structure of the situation did seem at least somewhat promising for me in the long term—there was no senior faculty member in my specialty, and sooner or later a tenured appointment in the field would have to be made—everyone recognized that. This was not lost on me—or on anyone else, including my junior colleagues, who arrived just as buoyed by their graduate experiences at the University of Chicago or Oxford as I had been by mine at Princeton, and just as ambitious and determined.

So my situation in the department was promising—and, at the same time, almost unbearably pressured. I was young—very young. I was not even finished with my dissertation. Yet senior colleagues were talking to me about earning tenure at Harvard. No one stopped to think that perhaps those conversations could best wait a bit. No one stopped to think that they might scare the daylights out of me.

One of my best friends on the junior faculty, Ethel Klein, who arrived soon after I did, characterized the game this way: "A man says to his wife, I'm going to divorce you, but you know, if you lose twenty pounds, and have a facelift, and become a gourmet cook, and get a better job and earn twice as much money so we can buy a bigger house, I might reconsider." Ethel and I had overlapped at Michigan; she had been a first-year graduate student there when I was in my senior year, and we shared Kent Jennings as an advisor. She researched and taught about women and politics, and she knew how to think about interpersonal power dynamics in smart and clever ways. She eventually gave up academia entirely and started a very successful polling firm.

Scarlett, on the other hand, was not quite as savvy, and academia felt like the only way forward.

My first semester of teaching was spring term, 1978, which began with one of Boston's worst-ever blizzards. For a few days classes were canceled, and I went stir-crazy, more than ready to get going but unable even to get to my office because of the snow. Eventually the city returned to normal and I taught two courses: a graduate seminar on constitutional interpretation, and an undergraduate course on comparative constitutional law.

The undergraduate course went well, although standing at a lectern in front of Harvard undergraduates was daunting, and I was very glad Bob Tucker had given me a chance to stand at the lectern at Princeton.

The graduate seminar was rocky. At a place as status-driven as Harvard, there is a natural tension between graduate students and junior faculty. The graduate students measure themselves against you, and they know you are the hired help. They're here to work with the famous senior faculty, not with you. But, since there was no senior scholar in my specialty, if they wanted to qualify in this field, they had to make do with me. And constitutional law was a natural choice for many students in American politics and political theory. It was a staple of undergraduate curricula everywhere, so an ability to teach it was useful for the job market. Some were also genuinely interested. One or two of the grad students that first semester are still friends and colleagues; not so long ago I sent a condolence note to one about the death of her husband. I served as the second reader of her dissertation, as I did for a few others along the way.

Other grad students that first semester were difficult. A secretary reported that one young woman made fun of the fact that I had a bad cold and so was not in the office one day. "He's awfully frail, isn't he," she said.

* * *

The New York Hilton, Labor Day, 1978. I had finished and defended my dissertation the previous spring, and I am going to my first major academic conference, the annual meeting of the American Political Science Association. I take the train from Boston to New York and check into the hotel. It is the first time I have stayed in such an expensive hotel by myself, but Harvard will pay for the room. It is the last time the Association will ever meet in New York; members are finding it too expensive.

Standing in line to check in, I see Bruce Murphy, who is another member of the panel on which I will appear. We say hello, we banter, we go to the Stage Delicatessen for dinner. Bruce and I have used some of the same materials in our dissertations, have met before.

The panel is the next morning. I present a snapshot of my dissertation, a summary of my argument about Justice Frankfurter. It is the first time I have presented any part of my argument to anyone beyond my dissertation committee or at job interviews, and as I speak I am thinking of the only other academic conference I have attended.

In the spring of my first year in graduate school, Fred Greenstein had arranged for me and another graduate student to attend a conference on psychology and politics at Yale. We drove half the night to get to New Haven and slept on the floor of my college housemate Edie's apartment.

The Yale conference was full of famous names and I was awestruck. One of the famous names, a discussant on one of the panels, savagely attacked the work of another member of the panel. He was vicious, unrelenting. It was my first exposure to such behavior, to academic warfare, and I paid close attention.

Be careful, I think. Be very careful.

So at my first American Political Science Association a few years later, in Manhattan, I am extremely nervous. But I speak steadily when I present my paper and answer questions with a degree of authority that surprises me. As I talk I think to myself, "I actually know what I'm talking about."

The panel has three discussants, senior scholars who will comment on the papers. All three praise my work, and I am startled yet again. One of them, Philippa Strum, will become a lifelong friend.

After the panel I am exhilarated; it has been a success—no attacks. Those would come later, when my work is published. But for now, at the New York Hilton on Labor Day weekend in 1978, I am a success, and I am happy, very happy. The panel is early in the conference, which leaves me several more days to enjoy New York. I mingle more at the conference, go to some cocktail parties, schmooze. I have never been so social, so extraverted in an academic setting—in any setting, really—and I wonder if this is a new me. I feel anything but frail.

* * *

When I got back to Cambridge, I needed to find a new place to live; my first apartment on Beacon Hill was not working out. I found a small but charming studio on Mt. Vernon Street, in the same neighborhood, just off Charles Street, the second floor of an old townhouse, with built-in bookshelves.

One afternoon as I was painting with the door open to let in some air, my upstairs neighbor passed by and introduced herself. She asked me what I did.

"You know," she said, "people say this was once Louie Brandeis's townhouse."

Electricity ran through me. Later that day I ran to the library, paint stains still on my clothes, to look it up. 114 Mt. Vernon St. was indeed the townhouse Brandeis bought while practicing law in Boston, before his appointment to the Supreme Court.

Well well well.

Once settled in the new apartment, I decided I needed to do something to challenge Harvard's coldness and find more of a place for myself. I would make myself indispensible, move myself to the center of the department's business: I volunteered to be Head Tutor.

The Head Tutor was the person in charge of the undergraduate honors and advising program. The department had many majors and a large number of graduate teaching fellows, so this was a big job—it counted as half of one's teaching load—and a complex one. There was a secretary, an office bureaucracy to manage, and assistant head tutors to appoint from among the graduate students. The job also meant interacting with central Harvard administrators, and it meant being in the office every day.

Although it could be trying at times, especially when dealing with high-maintenance students, I mostly enjoyed the job. I enjoyed advising students. I liked the buzz of a busy office. I enjoyed working with Sid Verba. Being busy in this way helped disguise the fact that the life of an academic is essentially a solitary life—one spends hours and hours alone, reading, writing, typing, preparing classes, doing one's research, reading in one's field. And being Head Tutor did mean much more interaction with my colleagues, senior and junior, than I would have had otherwise—they needed to go through me to get the Teaching Fellows they wanted, or to get an exception to policy for an undergraduate.

While running the tutorial office, I needed to start thinking, fast, about publishing my dissertation. On this front, the appointment at Harvard worked miracles.

Martin Kessler, editor-in-chief of Basic Books, contacted me, and we met at that first APSA conference. His invitation seemed to drop out of the sky.

We had lunch. He said he would be delighted to publish the dissertation, more or less as it was. He offered me an advance. As he spoke, all I could think was, "you mean you're going to pay me to publish this, I don't have to pay you?" At the time, Basic Books was a major social science publisher, and, as a trade publisher, working with them meant the possibility of more reviews and a larger readership. It was perfect.

Neither of these things—that first APSA panel, the publisher— would have happened, or happened in the way that they happened, had I not been a new Harvard faculty member. Being there, even as junior faculty, signaled to the rest of the professional world that this person was ok, smart, had done good work, was worth taking a look at. Attention would be paid—and for that I was, and am, eternally grateful.

But there was also a downside to this good fortune, I now see. When opportunities come to you, you do not learn some of the skills a professional academic needs to sustain a career. When people come to you, you do not think about making your own contacts, putting yourself on the conference circuit. When an APSA panel falls into your lap, you do not learn how to write a proposal for a paper or how to put together a panel, or even that there is a need to do so. When a major publisher offers you a contract straight out of the gate, you do not learn how to make your work known, cultivate editors, write a book proposal—how to sell yourself. You are pre-sold.

None of this occurred to me at the time, of course. And since I had already left graduate school, did not do a post-doc, and was in a place where senior faculty were extraordinarily busy and not particularly interested in mentoring their junior colleagues, I was, for many years, curiously naïve in the ways of academia, the nuts and bolts of being a professional.

The Harvard emphasis on smartness—on lunch table conversation, on being quick and insightful over a drink, on being generally well read, well-informed, cultured—reinforced this neglect of professional skills. If what seemed to be important was the ephemeral quality of smartness, then learning how to write an APSA panel proposal or getting oneself on the conference circuit, or learning how to talk to a book editor, were relatively unimportant details. If reading widely beyond one's specialty, seeing the latest art film or play or reading the latest literary sensation—things I greatly enjoyed anyway—were valued, that meant less time becoming a specialist, an expert, on a narrow set of topics.

This neglect of professional skills in favor of a more general intellectuality was a part of the Princeton program when I was there, and was exacerbated by the fact that its graduate curriculum had been a bit behind the times, especially in American politics. Princeton's program emphasized historical, institutional, and psychological analysis at a time when the rest of the discipline was rapidly abandoning such approaches in favor of what was considered more scientific methodology. Even large-scale empirical data collection—the Michigan brand of political science, with which I was quite familiar—was no longer considered cutting edge. The discipline moved toward supposedly predictive model-building based on the assumption of general rationality—people, including voters and politicians, have interests, and they rationally pursue and protect them—a dubious assumption, especially to anyone who has ever studied individual or group psychology. Political theorist Stephen Holmes, who was a junior colleague at Harvard, calls the approach "motivational reductionism."

From the distance of several decades, it's relatively easy to point out that the underlying theoretical assumptions and methods of political science underwent a profound shift during the Seventies—roughly speaking, from psychology to economics. The kinds of political analysis that had most interested me, both as an undergraduate and graduate student, and that had been dominant in the discipline, had psychological assumptions at their base: the Michigan model of voting (based on party identification, a social-psychological phenomenon); the political socialization of children; leadership, personality and politics; the study of political consciousness in revolutions and social movements, and in some political philosophy (Alexis de Tocqueville's analysis of American democracy, for example, relies a great deal on dissecting the American mind, and psychology is crucial in Hobbes); interpersonal relations on the Supreme Court; judicial and presidential biography (both LBJ and Nixon had, obviously, personality issues that played a huge role in what happened during their administrations).

All of this was shifting to supposedly more rigorous economic assumptions, and subfields and genres relying on the old methodologies were demoted. The discipline changed dramatically, but it took some departments (Princeton and Harvard among them) time to catch up. The old assumptions and methods didn't disappear, but they were no longer dominant, no longer where the action was.

So while graduate students in other programs in American politics were concentrating on data sets and ever more sophisticated mathematical modeling, Fred Greenstein's seminar on American politics started with Tocqueville and James Sterling Young's *The Washington Community*, which looks at interpersonal relations in early Washington, just as the city was being built in the first part of the nineteenth century. In Walter Murphy's public law seminar we read legal cases, concentrated on interpretive questions, and didn't go near empirical studies of Supreme Court voting records.

All this was much to my liking, but gave me a skewed impression of what my discipline was about. Similarly, judicial biography was rapidly becoming passé, as many scholars in public law, as my subfield is called, were also turning to model building and data collection. Personality and politics as a field was also on the way out, since you couldn't write an equation about or attach numbers to a leader's personality, and the quirks of personality were the exact opposite of the rational pursuit of well-defined interests.

The inferiority complex about whether the discipline of political science was a true "science" underlay much of this push toward supposedly more rigorous methodology. The new work sometimes yielded insight, but all in all was not my cup of tea, for it seemed to me more and more removed from the actualities of politics. The new style was spectacularly impressive technically, but often said very little about the real, messy world of politics, which in the end seemed to me driven by ideologies and personalities that were anything but rational. Hordes of scholars were developing formal models of interactions in Congress and state legislatures, or deriving ever-more sophisticated models of voting, but in the meantime, the American economy was melting down, Washington seemed unable to cope, and the far right wing was beginning to take over the Republican party in the person of a former Hollywood actor (and not a very good one at that). From my perspective, rationality was nowhere to be found. Even a real economist like Alan Greenspan was later belatedly forced to admit that economic actors (let alone political actors) do not always behave rationally, and that his assumption that they would do so while he chaired the Federal Reserve guided his policy choices and helped plunge us into the greatest economic crisis since the Great Depression.

So neither by training nor inclination was I a terribly well-prepared professional academic—yet there I was at Harvard. Fewer and fewer panels on American politics at the annual APSA meeting were of interest to me—or to many others, as it turned out, who eventually revolted against the discipline's scientific trend in a reform movement known as "perestroika" that erupted in the APSA in 2000. But for several decades, the decades in which I was a young scholar, the wind was blowing in a particular direction, and that wind was most definitely not at my back. More and more, I had to steady myself against the gusts.

I was an intellectual, certainly, maybe even a scholar, but I was not a scientist, and I didn't want to become one.

Instead of American politics, at least as studied by the new methodologies, what did interest me, more and more, was political theory—political philosophy—and gaining a firmer grounding in it would take some time. I am a much better scholar for having cultivated this interest—and even a better teacher, able to teach a wider range of courses—but the problem was the calendar. When you are a young professor at Harvard, or any institution of stature, you are assumed to have your scholarly interests fully formed the moment you begin, and you are supposed to go from one research project to another without stopping. You are not supposed to continue general reading to expand your disciplinary reach. You are expected to produce new work in your specialty at a steady clip.

And then there was teaching. Day to day, week to week, that is what we did, and, if we let it, it absorbed a great deal of time and energy.

It is one of the great puzzles of academic life that teaching matters so little at America's great universities. It mattered to some Princeton faculty, somewhat, but not nearly as much as scholarship and professional standing—and Princeton was an exception. At Harvard, some of my colleagues, senior and junior, were good or even great undergraduate teachers, but if it happened it happened almost as an accident, because someone performed well at the lectern, had a personality that transmitted itself, brought the material alive, like Sam Beer (having British manners and speech, as Sam did, certainly helped).

No one at Harvard ever asked me how things were going in the classroom. When I once tried to start a discussion of teaching methods at one of the department's monthly faculty dinners, eyes glazed over, people looked away. The subject was quickly changed. Conversations were never about how the department could improve teaching or whether the undergraduate curriculum as a whole worked or had any real coherence. Faculty members were independent contractors, teaching more or less what they wanted, the way they wanted.

No one's career at Harvard depended on their classroom performance. Dreadful teaching—truly dreadful—might hurt you when it came time for promotion to associate professor, but beyond that, no one cared. It just didn't matter. Although I was never in the room when senior appointments were discussed, I cannot imagine that any time was ever spent discussing how good a teacher a prospective senior colleague might be. At one point, Harvard appointed someone with whom I had worked at Princeton. A senior colleague at Harvard called me into his office and asked me what I thought of him. I began talking positively about his teaching—I had taken his graduate seminar. "No, no," my Harvard colleague interrupted, annoyed. "We don't care about his teaching. What do you think of his work?" "Work" of course did not include the classroom.

Scholarship, and academic reputation, were what counted. The bottom line, at least at Harvard: Were you *smart*, yes or no? And could you translate that smartness into work the world would notice? Hundreds of students, each paying a small fortune, perhaps going deeply into debt, may sit in a lecture hall at 2:00 p.m., but that morning and the night before, and the previous weekend, and during the last vacation, the professor who shows up to talk for fifty minutes, perhaps through a microphone because the class is so large, was drafting or revising an article or book chapter, or doing the reading for their next project, or reading some other scholar's paper so that they could comment on it at the next conference panel. State governments may give hundreds of millions of dollars to their universities, and alumni may give similar sums to private institutions, because these institutions are educating their children, future citizens, but the education of those undergraduates is way, way down on the list of what faculty members care about, if they care at all. Many do not. The dirty truth is that some of Harvard's most stellar scholars were mediocre teachers.

The retort of the higher education establishment to these plain facts is always this: That scholarship enriches teaching, that it takes an excellent scholar to be an excellent teacher. There is a tiny amount of truth in this, but far less than those who defend the status quo would like the public to believe. Classes in which our own current research can figure, can be presented to students, are relatively rare, and, for many members of the faculty, non-existent. My work on Felix Frankfurter gave me insight into the workings of the Supreme Court during the decades in which he sat on it, and that very occasionally led to a brief comment or two I could make when a class discussed a specific case. But my work on Frankfurter, which lasted five years, was hardly important to teaching a good class on American constitutional law.

And, of course, time is zero sum, an elementary truth that the higher ed establishment glosses over. If one spends hours each day preparing classes or (heaven forbid) grading papers or talking to students, that's hours not spent doing one's own work. And scholarly research and writing can take up every ounce, not only of time, but of energy. As I was finishing my dissertation, I said to a friend, "I wonder if it's possible to be a scholar and a human being at the same time."

The friend to whom I said this, Deb, was my housemate from Ann Arbor. She was just starting a graduate program in Russian history at Columbia as I was finishing my dissertation. Deb was also trying to sustain a new romance.

She's been a human being this fall, and feels her work at Columbia has suffered,

I recorded in my journal. She dropped out of Columbia. I pushed on at Harvard.

Time, time, time—is fleeting. No time to write here, no time to read the New York Times. No time.

Zero sum. And for most academics, sooner or later, something has to give. What gives, more often than not, is teaching. One of my Harvard colleagues—someone who actually earned tenure from within—said at one department meeting: "Of course, the courses we give our first year of teaching are the courses we give for the rest of our lives. . . ." Everyone chuckled: an elementary truth. We prepare lectures once, then repeat them, and repeat them. Why prepare new ones?

Many do care more about teaching at smaller colleges—a few care deeply—but even at a small college, scholarship is still the ticket to a future. And faculty members everywhere are not writing their next article or book so that it will enrich their future classroom performance, or the classroom performance of anyone else. Their status in their discipline, their standing, their future, will not depend on their teaching. It simply does not matter to their professional colleagues, so it does not matter much to them, either.

Why, I've asked myself many times, did I continue to let it matter to me, when the signals I received were crystal clear that this was a mistake? According to many of my senior colleagues, it was even a mistake to become Head Tutor—just as undergraduate teaching didn't count, undergraduate administration didn't count either. This was of course great hypocrisy; someone had to run the Tutorial office. The department couldn't function without someone doing the job. And, unlike some other departments, the Government department at the time always assigned the job to a junior faculty member (which was, of course, quite convenient for the senior faculty).

But why did I care so much?

There's no doubt that I simply enjoyed the high of being a popular teacher—and still do. It was, and is, quite a high. A graduate student at Harvard once told me that she was at a dinner with some undergraduates where faculty members were discussed. "Let's face it, he's a god," one of them said about me, and the others nodded. Annie Wilson, James Q's daughter, took one of my courses and, I later discovered, told her father I was the best teacher in the college.

Heady stuff. Hard to resist if, in fact, you have the teaching gene.

But there was more to it than simple ego, or at least, that's what I've told myself, semester after semester, year after year.

Famed feminist bell hooks describes school, for her, as "the place of ecstasy—pleasure and danger"— the place where she could forget, transcend the racism she faced and her modest surroundings and reinvent herself. Similarly, Jay Parini writes of his more privileged life, "I found myself being articulate in a classroom, discussing matters that felt dear and relevant to my intellectual and spiritual life." And, he adds, "the intensity of this experience was transforming."

So it was for me. The classroom was the only steady home I had known since I was thirteen, and even before that, from the first day of first grade, doing well in school was what I knew how to do. It was what I *did*. There was the preprogramming of my Jewish genes, what George Steiner calls the instinctive preference for teaching and learning. There was the ferment of my extended family, arguing, always arguing, as I grew up, and my parents' love of reading. There was their divorce and the convoluted reality of their second marriages, from which I needed refuge. There was my complete lack of interest in sports, and, at least until I safely had a PhD, there was the need not to think much about or do anything about that nagging matter of my sexuality.

And so the classroom was home. It had always meant so much to me, been so important to me as a person, in every phase of my life, that, once I became the person standing at the front of the class, what I did there seemed more important than any article or even book I might write. It might not be every student who had the same kind of experience as I had had in my classroom—it might be only a handful in any given class—but they mattered. And if I was a good enough teacher, I could perhaps make it happen for some of the others, or make them see themselves and the world a bit differently.

As I saw it, that was the essence of my job. I wanted to wake my students up in the way I had been woken up. I wanted them to argue with me and with each other. I wanted them to learn how to have an opinion and defend it. I wanted to push them left if they leaned right and push them right if they leaned left. I wanted to shake them up if they were complacent or help them learn how to discipline themselves if they were out of control. I wanted them to be so excited about what they were thinking that I had to shut them up so that others could speak. I wanted them to grow.

This course made me think I could go to law school.

This course made me change my career goals.

I went home for Christmas and told my parents they were wrong about abortion.

This class really taught me how to speak up.

When I heard things like this—all of these from notes I received in my first few years of teaching—notes I still have in a yellowing, crumbling folder—I felt I had accomplished something of value.

A woman named Melissa worked as a staff member in one of the science departments at Harvard, and enrolled in one of my courses. After class one day she mentioned she was thinking about law school, and asked for advice about where to apply. She didn't know if she'd be able to manage it financially, she said, she'd have to work her way through. I suggested she look at Northeastern in Boston, which makes it easier than most law schools to earn income while studying.

A few years after I left Harvard, I got a letter from Melissa, thanking me for my advice. She did indeed go to Northeastern. She did well, met a man there she married, and when she graduated, clerked for a federal judge.

That letter meant the world to me, more than the article I published that year. No one reads that article anymore, but Melissa still has her life and her career. So do David Sanger and Nick Kristof, whose senior theses I advised, both now major journalists at the *New York Times*, and so do many others.

So I did put a good deal of time and energy into teaching and advising. And I enjoyed being Head Tutor. Being able to advise students and help them with their academic problems seemed like useful work—and it was certainly more lively than being shut up alone in a library all day.

Each September, the Harvard *Crimson* published the "Confi Guide," a funny and often spot-on review of various professors and courses. The first day it was available for sale was the first day freshmen moved into their dorms in Harvard Yard, always a Saturday. I would rush to the Yard, excited, anxious, to buy a copy. I was as nervous riding the Red Line to the yard that first Saturday as it had during my job interview. I was thrilled, absolutely thrilled, when I read a glowing review.

On dark days, Miss Scarlett would later wonder: Did she put time and effort into teaching because she didn't have the right stuff to be a first-rate scholar, perhaps because she was lazy? There were certainly days when that seemed to have truth in it, when her eyes glazed over reading the *Harvard Law Review*, evenings when she actually went to a movie rather than sit at a typewriter (these wonderful machines we used to have). But then Miss Scarlett would think: Well, didn't I get through graduate school and produce a dissertation in record time? Certainly someone who was lazy wouldn't have been able to do that. And didn't the dissertation win a prize (a prize given by the APSA, named, of course, for Corwin)? Laziness or a lack of brains didn't seem to be a problem.

When Basic Books published the Frankfurter volume in the spring of 1981, it received wide attention and was reviewed everywhere, including the front page of the *Washington Post Bookworld* and in the *New York Times* (on the same Sunday—quite a weekend). A friend of a friend, now a very well-known scholar, later startled me by calling the book a literary success. Some of the first reviews were laudatory, some were negative, which wasn't a surprise; the methodology was controversial. But it was new—a psychological study of a Supreme Court justice, an innovation, and Frankfurter was an important figure. I was twenty-nine when it was published. So no, laziness didn't seem to be the problem, and the world was certainly paying attention to my work . . . exactly what Harvard expected.

The attention the Frankfurter book received was amazing. It appeared in the window of several Cambridge bookstores, and I had to blink several times when I first saw it there. Dita called me at home excitedly one Sunday morning to ask if I had seen the *Boston Globe* (I hadn't)—George Higgins had written a column about the book. The Government department shared a building with the Economics department at the time, and even the economists seemed to suddenly know who I was (Basic Books had published an ad with a small photo of me), and they started nodding in the hall as I walked to the bathroom. Larry Summers even turned down the music when I asked him to (he had the office one floor below mine, and we both often worked early in the morning). There was even an adulatory review in *Time*.

So for a while, Miss Scarlett floated on air. And despite the social chilliness of her senior colleagues, there were many things about Harvard to enjoy. Cambridge often has an Indian Summer, and on those warm fall days I would buy a bag lunch and sit on the steps of Memorial Church, across the Yard from Widener library. There were junior members of the department who became friends and true colleagues, especially political theorist Nancy Rosenblum, a close friend to this day; we still sometimes read drafts of each other's work. There were senior common room lunches at Leverett House—both Sid and Dita were affiliates, made sure I was invited to join.

One perfect, sunny fall day, the famous, erudite historian John Clive, nearing the end of his career, told stories over a Senior Common Room lunch at Leverett about touring London with T.S. Elliott. Around the table listening were distinguished members of at least six other departments, including a visiting Nobel Prize winner. There was wine and good food. After lunch I had to stop at Widener for a book, and walking out the front entrance, down the long steps to the Yard on a perfect, warm afternoon, I felt as if I were living a dream. That night I asked in my journal:

Could anything be better than this?

John Rawls—John Rawls!—probably the most important political theorist of the twentieth century, a member of the Philosophy department, about whom I had written one of my seminar papers at Princeton, called me at home and invited me to lunch; he needed some references about free speech. We had lunch several times, in fact, and Rawls often brought a tomato from home in his jacket packet, which he munched on as we talked.

Jeez. A bit like John Stuart Mill asking for advice.

I was promoted to Associate Professor, which, at Harvard, is an untenured position, adding three years to your contract, for a total of eight.

To be sure, there were times when my status was made clear. One day there was a meeting of faculty, senior and junior, in American politics, to organize some sort of new research center. We met in a very small conference room with few chairs. One by one, some senior members arrived late, and there weren't enough chairs. Each time, those already in the room looked at me, making it clear it was my job to surrender my chair and go to the classroom next door and fetch another one.

This happened several times. Since those arriving were all able-bodied men, I wondered why they couldn't get their own chairs, but I did what the glances told me to do. My friend Ethel, already in the room, later told me that Jim Wilson said at one point, while I was fetching yet another chair, "one more chair and we'll have to get him a union card."

Another junior colleague once said about Jim, "You know, you have to be careful when you bend down to kiss his feet that you don't cut your forehead on the crease in his pants"—and, funny as that is and was meant to be, it captures something of the flavor of senior-junior relations at Harvard.

But for the most part, weeks and months went by without gross reminders of rank. Classes were going well, and there was much to enjoy: guest lectures, smart colleagues, the general Cambridge buzz, which attracted visitors for long and short stays from everywhere. People said if you stood still in Harvard Square, sooner or later practically everyone you knew in academia would walk by, and it was close to true.

And then? And then the Harvard tide turned.

I had been on the fast track since starting college—since high school, really. All along I had been following all the implicit instructions bright students glean from their surroundings, and had no qualms about what I was doing—the instructions felt right, natural. Nothing felt amiss, and I seemed to be in that blissful state where I could happily do what the world requires. Get all As in high school. Check (except for chemistry). Do a lot of extracurricular activities. Check. Get into a good college. Check. Work hard, do honors, graduate *summa*. Check. Do internships. Check. Get into a major graduate program, impress the faculty. Check. Choose an audacious dissertation. Check. Get a good job at a prestigious place. Check. Publish your dissertation. Check. Hope that it makes a splash. Check.

It was as if I had been on automatic pilot. And then the instructions seemed to stop, abruptly, and suddenly I didn't know how to fly the plane.

OK guys, now what?

No answer.

Hello? Anyone home?

Silence.

You mean I have to figure this out by myself? And, by the way, why am I on this track moving at the speed of light? It seems to have accelerated recently—shouldn't it be slowing down a bit?

Silence.

Um . . . can't you just give me a hint at what should come next?

At the vast majority of American universities, the book on Frankfurter combined with a strong teaching and service record would have been enough to earn tenure, and I would have been able to relax, to take a bit of time to figure out what came next. But Harvard was different—and I certainly knew that going in. Harvard required two books for tenure, or so the official line went at the time (a rule ignored when it suited the powers that be) and a second, quick book seemed not to be in the cards for me. I had been running so fast for so long that I needed to slow down, catch up, both in life and as a scholar.

And I took a detour for a while, disastrously, as I started thinking about a second project. Given my growing interest in political theory, I wanted to write a theoretical analysis of how the Supreme Court treated marginal people and groups—the disabled, the mentally ill, children, gays and lesbians, the poor, aliens and immigrants. My material would be cases, mostly Supreme Court cases. The book would be commentary, analysis, just like many books in the field before and after. But Dita took me to lunch and told me no, that couldn't possibly be my next project. She was quite certain about that. She uttered the three worst words in the English language for an academic—"It's been done." Do something about lawyers, how cases get to court, she suggested. It was an off-hand comment, the kind Dita often made, but I was so desperate to find my bearings that I listened. Whether she was speaking for herself or for her colleagues was unclear, but I was being told to make myself into a more empirical political scientist.

For the first time, the life instruction coming from on high seemed wrong, out of kilter, didn't feel right, didn't feel like me.

Yet I stupidly put aside what I wanted to work on and spent roughly eighteen months trying to work up a project about lawyers—background reading, early interviews. My heart wasn't in it, and, unsurprisingly, I got nowhere. It seemed to me everything there was to know about lawyers was well studied already (here was a field where "it's been done" truly applied). I went back to my original idea, and it eventually bore fruit, but these were the worst possible eighteen months for someone in my situation to flap about on an abandoned project. At the very point in my career where I needed to be most confident, most sure of what I was doing if I wanted a perch on the "A" list, I was just the opposite.

So I am in trouble. I am stumbling around on a second project and, worse still, after the first few months of reviews and publicity, there seem to be second thoughts about my book on Frankfurter. "It was a literary success," Dita said at another lunch, "not a scholarly success."

Ah.

Because it was a psychological biography and less than admiring, it was perceived by some as an attack on an iconic figure. Frankfurter had been a professor of law at Harvard, accustomed to being treated with deference, accustomed to being the smartest person in the room, at least in his own mind, even when the room was in the White House, where he advised FDR. But when appointed to the Court, he was one of nine, equal to the other eight, and the lack of deference, the inability to maneuver behind the scenes, which was his style, the failure to persuade, drove him nearly mad, and this led him to harden his positions, to move farther to the right. As I saw it, he found himself isolated, unhappy, on the wrong side of history.

This was not a popular argument among members of the legal establishment, to say the least, and so there were some savage reviews in law journals, which took a while to appear (my favorite line was from arch-conservative Robert Bork's review: this was a "better book than Hirsch intended"). Some newspapers called the book brilliant and the *New Yorker* said I was "a good writer," and there were some good reviews in academic journals, but the Frankfurter posse, as I came to think of them, was after me, and my early sheen was now tarnished.

And having been rushed, willingly, pantingly, through graduate school, my knowledge of my field was still forming, and I needed time to catch up. But the Harvard clock was ticking. There needed to be a second project, fast.

Is that my Harvard story? The lawyers didn't like my first project, and I had a slow, rough start on my second? That is the story but it is not the only story. My father had died at sixty-one—the most poignant moment in a man's life, Freud calls it—just as I was finishing the Frankfurter book. And, not coincidentally, I had finally realized that being attracted to men was not a phase. A different kind of life beckoned, needed to be created, from scratch.

So instead of burrowing back into the library, for the first time in my life I am taking time off, exploring gay Boston, still a year or two away from the plague. I am drinking so much Perrier in gay bars, in fact, I should have been given the Legion of Honor by the French government.

Life and career are not in synch; there really is no second project. I teach, teach well, but the rest of my energy is going elsewhere.

I am depressed, I am anxious. I am drinking wine at dinner, listening to Ella Fitzgerald and Sarah Vaughn. I try to work but I can't work. I am in trouble.

* * *

July 1983. One blistering hot Friday in July, sweating in the stacks of Widener library, I decide I cannot take it anymore. I pack a bag and go to North Station and get on a train for Manchester, a town north of Boston with a beautiful beach and a lively restaurant near the train station.

On the train, I am near tears. My career, derailed, the unrelenting heat, my father's death, my so-far timid attempts to find gay life.

I had tossed a paperback into my bag. *The Wapshot Chronicles* by John Cheever. I begin to read.

I cannot stop reading. Cheever is writing about the landscape through which the train is traveling, the landscape of declining but proud New England families, the long slow decline producing eccentric characters both funny and sad. The writer's skill is amazing to me, captures me completely.

I am in trouble but I have brought a book. By the time I get to the beach, I am smiling, and the sea breeze is cool. And that night, back in Boston, still smiling, instead of watching a movie I take myself to a gay bar, and actually speak to someone.

* * *

My social world was opening up, finally, but meanwhile, the powers that be were continuing to have second thoughts about my so-far brilliant career—and so was I. The Harvard Law School found numerous ways of attacking my book. They printed not one but two negative reviews in the same issue of their law review, without giving me the opportunity to respond. Then, in 1982, the law school invited me to a conference on the 100th anniversary of Frankfurter's birth. I was put on a panel chaired by one of the people who had written one of the two scathing reviews (Harvard lawyers always play fair, of course) and other members of the law faculty, some from the ranks of Frankfurter's law clerks, showed up to cross-examine me from the audience. They ignored the other members of the panel and fired hostile question after hostile question at me.

"Why didn't you interview Paul Freund about Frankfurter, he knew him well?"

"Actually, I did. I have him answering my questions on tape . . . would you like to hear it?"

Most of the audience laughed, but my interlocutor looked like he wanted to kill me. It was unmistakable, and not subtle: the Law School did not like my work, did not like it at all. I had a similar experience at Yale, where I was invited to address a faculty colloquium: a lovely dinner at Mory's and then unrelenting cross-examination. At a time in my career when I should have been currying favor with the lions of the legal profession, I was, if not quite Public Enemy #1, certainly on the list of the Ten Most Wanted.

So between the determined opposition of elite law professors and my own floundering on a second project, tenure was not in the cards. Disaster had struck; Scarlett had gone from the belle of the ball to ruined woman, forced to tear down the drapery material and use it for her dresses.

I would have to leave Harvard, leave Boston in just a few short years. How did this happen? I was shaken up, more shaken than I had been since my parents' divorce, and I couldn't quite absorb what was happening. Didn't the dissertation win a prize? Didn't the *New York Times* call the book brilliant?

* * *

I learn for certain that I will have to leave at lunch with Dita (where else?) in 1984. I ask her, point blank, whether I have a chance at tenure; the question can no longer be avoided. "Look," she says, and I know immediately, even before she finishes her first sentence. "Look" is always followed by bad news. Look, the job is not going to work out. Look, our relationship is over, I'm moving out. Look, I have bad news, the cyst is cancerous, you need surgery.

Look. Pay attention. Your life is about to change.

Dita is famous for making snap judgments, and many times I have witnessed this, heard her dismiss a colleague or a graduate student with one withering sentence or a shrug. "A heart is no substitute for a head," she once remarked about a colleague, a much-celebrated scholar at Berkeley, more left-leaning than she. "Not house-broken" was her simple comment about another colleague, who, sure enough, became engulfed by scandal within a few years. Her division of the academic world was simple: those worth her time, those not.

While I'm listening to Dita move me from one category to the other, I steal glances around the dingy basement café off Harvard Square that she seems to love, for unknown reasons, since the food is dreadful, pulled pork sandwiches and tall espresso drinks in dirty glasses. I wonder how many more times I will be here, how many more times I will ride the Red Line to Beacon Hill.

Dita talks on. Small beads of sweat begin trickling down my armpit, and a thin line of sweat forms at my temples, but I say little and remain outwardly calm, the kind of calm Lillian Hellman describes as coming only in moments of great danger. Life's small glitches can send her into a rage, Hellman reports in her memoirs, but when momentous, life-changing events occur—when she learns she is being called to testify before HUAC at the height of the McCarthy madness—the House Un-American Committee—she feels absolute stillness.

I drink my espresso. Today is my HUAC; the TV cameras are rolling.

Dita is nervous as she speaks, stumbles over words, unusual for her. Perhaps she expects an argument or a tantrum. But I keep myself composed and my voice even. I say very little; there is no point in arguing. A decision has been made; the Chief Justice is announcing it. There is no appeal.

Two years later, when I somehow land a good job in a professionally respected department, a department containing many Harvard PhDs, Dita will take me to lunch again, this time at Cambridge's nicest restaurant. And later still, after I finally finish my second book, I will pass through Cambridge and we will meet for coffee at that same basement café, on a freezing and dark November afternoon. She will seem delighted to see me and will tell me how much she liked the book, starting to talk about it while she is still sitting down. She is all smiles, friendly and warm. That will be the last time I see her. When we were done we walked back into Harvard Square together, and I watched her disappear into the crowd. She will die a few months after that November day, of overwork, many thought.

But that November day is in the future, and at this lunch I cannot yet imagine it as I sit mostly silent in the basement café hearing her pronounce my fate.

After lunch I go . . . to a bookstore, and I see that Virginia Woolf's diaries, in hardcover, have been remaindered. I have never understood the Bloomsbury obsession but I am intrigued and I need diversion. I know I need not to think just yet about what has just happened, and the handsome diaries are so cheap. I buy the first two volumes and take the Red Line home, and begin reading.

I spend the next six days doing little but reading all five volumes, every word, every editor's footnote. I teach my classes, distractedly, but I cancel office hours, reschedule dinner with a friend, avoid the gym and the laundry, and read. Virginia is another strong woman (despite the breakdown she seemed to have each time she finished a book—which felt way too familiar) and I can see from her life, from her words, that there are different ways of being strong, that one can be weak at times but still strong overall, vibrant, creative.

One can move on.

I know I will not be able to put what I see in her words to immediate use. My crisis is too raw, too overwhelming. But I store away the lesson I take from my reading somewhere deep, a deposit to be withdrawn later, when I'm ready.

When I've read so much my eyes begin to blur, late in the evening, still not able to sleep, I watch movies, sometimes all night.

Soon, though, I had to face the reality that, for the first time in my academic life, I was not going to succeed. I was devastated. Flattened. After my Bloomsbury and movie binge, I stumbled about, wondering what would become of me.

Feeling guilty about my stumble at the start of a second project, I did not stop and think that this was how the system worked, stumble or no stumble, for almost everyone. Only a tiny fraction at Harvard made it through; at the time I was there, perhaps one in fifteen. Harvard brought you there, gave you a decent interval of time—just long enough to establish a life—and then expected you to go elsewhere.

But of course, bright PhDs who have been academic stars since grade school don't step back and analyze the situation dispassionately. They blame themselves, and go through a very hard time. They are thunderstruck. One by one I watched other junior faculty members come to this crisis in their careers and lives. All of them are now distinguished academics, yet every one of them went through a very rough patch. I watched more than one or two of them (mostly straight men) cry. One began drinking heavily. I called his wife and suggested therapy or AA; ten years later she thanked me.

Yet when my turn came, I had not learned a thing from having watched them, and I went through my own saga of self-doubt and recrimination. I did not understand what was happening to me, and I felt like a complete failure. I had been in the Ivy League for twelve years. Contemplating anything else, at that moment, felt like a demotion.

There was only one way to think about what lay ahead: Exile.

Of course, from this distance, it's easy to see the almost comic absurdity of this—from literary success to "failure" because I couldn't beat the odds in a system specifically designed to prevent the beating of the odds. And, from this distance, it's even easier to see the myopia with which we Ivy League junior faculty members evaluated our options, failing to recognize our extraordinary privilege. Any academic job at a decent institution was, for most PhDs, becoming harder and harder to come by.

But such is the power of a few prestigious institutions sitting at the top of a status-mad profession. Being forced to leave Mount Olympus, even when that is built into the way things work, is experienced as personal failing.

I started seeing a therapist, who believed in tough love and zen detachment (a strange combination). He was unsympathetic, and didn't help much on this front. "A person who wanted a job would work all the time," he told me, and of course between fear and angst, it was difficult to accomplish anything beyond teaching my classes. The same was true for the others I had watched go through this; every one of them said they reached a point where they just couldn't think straight enough to write anything, or even to read much. It was the same for me, and I spent a lot of time staring at blank walls.

The institution did nothing to ease the transition. No advice, no comforting talk with the chair or a dean or even senior colleagues. No pats on the back for a job well done, for all those spectacular teaching evaluations. Once I made clear I was not going to ask for a tenure vote (there was no point), it was, for the most part, as if I no longer existed. There was a discussion of a reform of the graduate curriculum at one department meeting and I spoke up about it. The next day a senior colleague told me I no longer had the right to speak at meetings. I stopped attending.

What a very few senior colleagues (including Jim Wilson) did do was try to be helpful on the job market. This was both gracious and self-interested. The system depended on Harvard's junior faculty moving on to good or at least decent jobs elsewhere. If the junior faculty could not be placed when they left, the system would collapse—few would accept a job if it meant, in the end, professional suicide. So while I appreciated the help, I also saw, even at the time, that it did not come entirely from altruism or from regard for me.

A junior colleague had said, when we talked about leaving, "I just want them to be wistful about me when I go." Were they wistful about any of us? Unlikely. In their view, we had been given the enormous gift of spending time among the elect, and that was that. There were plenty of new PhDs to take our place. Now, decades later, I am tempted to write: There is always plenty of cheap labor to be found. Junior salaries, after all, were a fraction of the salaries paid to senior stars, who had to be lured to Cambridge from attractive jobs elsewhere, often with a spouse who also needed some kind of job at the university.

I was especially unhappy at the prospect of leaving Boston. I had made a home for myself there, loved the city, finally, had close, intimate friends. The city suited me, and so for a brief time I even considered changing careers to make it possible to stay. This was partly desperation, partly inspiration, partly the kind of normal experimentation I had skipped while climbing the academic ladder.

When I asked myself what else I could do, I thought: Perhaps I could become a psychologist, work with the gay community, my community, decimated and devastated by AIDS.

Last night, business as usual, a social gathering turned into a discussion of AIDS. As usual, I go numb. Someone else is angry, someone is holding back tears. I am numb.

I finally understand about German Jews, the ones who stayed. What else can you do? What else is there to do but to cling to every shred of normalcy, of routine—of life? Every new piece of information is an assault.

. . .

I went to the hospital to see Duane, brought him ice cream, since that's all I could think of to bring, he's lost so much weight.

When I walked in one of the doctors was there, asking questions, recording information, trying hard to hide his disgust, not succeeding. The look on his face was more chilling than the letter to the editor in this week's New York Times, saying that everyone who is sick should be tattooed and rounded up.

I wondered how long it would take for someone to start talking about concentration camps. And this was the New York Fucking Times.

I don't think Duane's Harvard doctor would disagree. I went out into the hall to wait until the doctor was done, and when he left and I went back into the room, Duane, all 6 foot 2 of him, looked crumpled up, like he had been mugged and left for dead in an alley somewhere.

"Can you imagine what it's like in Oklahoma," he deadpanned, and we both tried to laugh.

Duane was actually from Oklahoma, had been active in Democratic party politics there, and had served on Rosalynn Carter's White House staff.

Month by month, friend by friend, I helplessly watched the death toll mount, and I wondered if a change of career would allow me to do something, anything, to help. Then, too, I had a strong interest in psychology, which followed naturally from my work on Frankfurter, and it seemed like that might provide a path. So, almost as a lark, I applied to the graduate program in clinical psychology at Boston University, at the same time as I began interviewing for other jobs in political science.

BU accepted me, to my surprise, and, with much trepidation, I enrolled for a month. Over Labor Day weekend in 1984 I attended the annual meeting of the American Political Science Association, as usual, and delivered a paper, interacted with colleagues as if everything were normal. Then on Tuesday morning I attended an orientation session for new graduate students at BU.

What on earth am I doing?

I asked in my journal early that morning. Did I really want to change careers? Could I really see years of classes, internships, another dissertation, then advanced training to become a clinical psychologist? Was I ready to turn my back on a discipline to which I had devoted more than a decade?

To the extent that I had any plan at all, I was going to pursue BU's program at the same time as I kept teaching full time at Harvard for my last two years. That was the only way to make things work financially— BU's tuition was very high, and they offered me no aid.

This wasn't a remotely viable plan. I would get up at 4:30 to finish reading for my BU classes, then rush around all day, shuttling to BU classes on the Green Line and then taking the Red Line to Harvard to teach, often going back and forth more than once a day. Constitutional Law at 11:00 (teaching) and Advanced Psychopathology at 2:00 (taking). Going back and forth between institutions, between disciplines, between being a student and being a professor, gave me a kind of vertigo. There was also an internship at BU, which involved attending and observing a group therapy session in the evening.

Although I had studied personality theory, I was woefully underprepared for a graduate program in psychology. I had taken only one psych course in college, and I remembered little of it. If I had been able to do school full time I might have been able to catch up, but leading the double life of a student and a professor seemed impossible.

And, perhaps decisively, I had not yet given up the idea that I belonged in academia, that perhaps I could land on my feet after Harvard. So I quickly dropped out of BU and pursued an academic job.

The job market was rough, in part because of those wasted eighteen months. I had finally turned to the sort of project I wanted to write, and had several early pieces of it done, but the whole thing wasn't yet hanging together, so it was difficult to talk about it in job seminars. As week after week passed in my last year at Harvard, as the New Year came and went with no job offer, it felt as if I was about to be thrown off the edge of a cliff.

At job seminars one presents a paper, but the possible-future-colleagues who are listening don't care so much about the specifics as the general: What's the overall argument here, what's the payoff, will there be a publishable book, how does this paper fit into the bigger picture—the answers to which I was not really sure. And of course, honesty in these situations is out of the question. One cannot say, "well, I've written this paper, and one or two others, but I'm not quite sure how this all fits together, where it's going, whether there's going to be a book or rather a series of articles, I need time to figure that out." The response would be: fine, figure it out on your own time.

Somehow, though, I muddled through, and pretended I had no doubts at all. There would be more publications out of the project, *of course* there would be.

Meanwhile, there were classes to finish up. I was incredibly emotional in my last semester. I wrote one last set of letters of recommendation through tears in an empty office, after the movers had packed up the books. During my final weeks in Boston I also managed somehow to pull a tendon in my leg, and was hobbling around on crutches yet again. I was a mess.

Eventually, though, a good job was offered and the tendon healed.

* * *

Summer, Ogunquit, Maine. An hour or two north of Boston, with a beautiful beach. A refuge. A quiet town, a haven for French Canadians, with a small gay colony. Charmingly, one hears French spoken at the beach, in a restaurant.

A cool and stormy Friday after many perfect sunny days. Because rain is coming, I sit on a bench under the long awning at the entrance to the beach to read, rather than venturing out onto the sand. I am reading an obscure and wonderful gay novel set in the 1920s in the South. I get lost in it.

A friend is driving down from Vermont so I go to the Inn to meet him. We met in graduate school, each gay but closeted, became good friends for a time, each of us tentatively finding our way to those places. First, the place where we can tell ourselves, then the place where we can tell others. It took longer back then, we both came of age in the late Sixties and early Seventies.

My friend wants to nap after his long drive, so I go back to the awning. The wind and surf are picking up, the breeze is cool and rain is definitely on the way. On the way back to the beach I stop and buy a lunch, chopped liver on rye and cream soda, things I never eat or drink at home, but today, for some reason, is different, today is special.

Back under the awning, a well-dressed, lovely young French Canadian mother sits down next to me with a beautiful child, and lifts her long skirt to wrap him against the wind. The child laughs and throws his toy out onto the sand, but the mother hesitates to pick it up, she will get sand on her lovely clothes. I retrieve the toy for them just as the drizzle starts. The mother smiles, thanks me. We chat a bit in French, the language I began taking in seventh grade. The little boy smiles at me.

I know that I will soon no longer live close to this place I love, I know that I will soon have to trade Boston for another place—but for this moment at least, protected by the awning, book in my lap, storm coming, good friend asleep at the Inn, it does not matter.

I go back to my novel. The mother and child are smiling at me. I look out at the ocean for a long time, and the rain begins. I will think often of how the wind felt that day, of the young mother and her child, of how she gracefully lifted her skirt to protect him.

Storms come and go, I think. Take shelter where you can.

Miss Scarlett headed west.

7

ACCOUNTING

Man is free only when he is doing what the deepest self likes, and knowing what the deepest self likes, ah! that takes some diving.

— D. H. Lawrence

To her surprise, Miss Scarlett loved California; in many ways it changed who she was. But she never felt truly at home in its gigantic university system, nor did she love the skin cancer the state's blazing sunshine gave her. For one thing, once the first lesion was successfully removed, it meant always wearing awkward, large hats with wide brims.

"You look like Katharine Hepburn in that hat," my friend Rob said when he saw me for the first time in one of those hats, walking up to the restaurant where we were meeting for lunch.

From then on, he called me Miss Kate.

* * *

The future Miss Kate spent her last night in Boston at the Park Plaza hotel. The next morning was a perfect summer day, warm sun, cool breeze. As I got into a cab and took the short ride to the airport, I watched the sunlight play among the trees of the Public Garden and began tearing up. I stayed teary all day, first on the plane to Dallas and then on the connecting flight to San Diego. The tears were for Boston: I was homesick even before the first plane took off.

Once I changed planes I sensed I was entering a different country. Gone were the crisp tailored clothes of Bostonians, replaced by the comfortable and sloppy shorts and tops of the American southwest. On one of the flights the film *Hoosiers* was shown, an incredibly corny but

103

effective story starring Gene Hackman and Barbara Hershey. Hackman comes to a small town in Indiana in the Fifties to teach and to coach its high school basketball team, and, against all odds, brings it to the state championship within his first year. A teacher moving to a new place . . . more tears.

The tears were for the city and the life I had just left, but also for the self I was leaving behind. For I could no longer play the ingénue, the young over-achiever, I realized half consciously on the planes carrying me from the East coast to the West. I could no longer think of myself as someone full of untested promise, which, as Vivian Gornick has pointed out, is one of the quintessential American personas. I was entering a new phase of my life, and I didn't know what it would look like— and so, as I did when I arrived at the University of Michigan, I felt for a moment as if I didn't exist. "California, for God sake," I muttered to myself as the plane descended to the San Diego airport—always a harrowing experience, since planes had to approach the runway so close to buildings and a freeway that a disaster seemed just a few inches away.

Had I crashed, or had I landed safely? As I got off the plane, rumpled and jet-lagged, I didn't have a clue.

My new colleague Peter Irons—irascible, smart, ornery, a former draft resister who had gone to jail—met me at the airport, took me straight to a Toyota dealership where I bought my first-ever car, what turned out later to be the only lemon among the millions of Toyotas zipping along California's freeways.

The sun was scalding. It was mid-July, and I had never felt sun so strong. Jet-lagged, anxiety-ridden, I went to the hotel where I planned to stay while I looked for an apartment, but it was horrid, run down, noisy, and I left immediately, driving my new Toyota around the city in a daze, looking for a place to stay. I spent that first night in a cheap motel just off I-5, the coastal freeway, in Pacific Beach, a neighborhood in between central San Diego and La Jolla, where the university was located.

I slept little, dozed a bit from 3:00 to 6:00 a.m., and when I opened my eyes and turned on the radio, heard a calm California voice announce that "we've had a small earthquake." I bolted out of bed, terrified. I opened the door and looked for rubble or signs of panic, but everything seemed more or less in place.

I started driving along the city's beach communities. It was early Sunday morning, around 6:30, and of course no one else was awake or outside. It felt a bit like driving through the movie *On the Beach*, after nuclear war. But the ocean was absolutely dazzling.

The Pacific was omnipresent in San Diego; even five or ten miles inland, one could still feel the crispness in the air. As P. D. James once described it, coastal Southern California is the most perfect climate on earth—the warm, dry sun of the desert cooled by constant ocean breezes. Los Angeles, 120 miles to the north, was more muggy and smoggy. San Diego and Santa Barbara, on either side of LA, were perfect, or as close to perfect as one could find.

The job did not feel so perfect.

Getting the offer from UC San Diego had not been smooth. They had interviewed me the year before, and were not enthusiastic enough to hire me immediately. The seminar at which I presented my work felt like a fistfight, in fact, as several members of the department interrupted the talk and shouted at me.

I had never experienced or witnessed anything like this sort of behavior in an academic setting. I was told later that this was typical for the political science department, which prided itself on its rigor, its standards, its toughness, its relentless cross-examination of any speaker. "They're a pack of Jewish wolves," a friendly sociologist called them, to my amazement. It felt like I had somehow landed in a strange, parallel universe.

It took fancy footwork by Irons, the other law scholar in the department, to persuade the department to hire me. We had met briefly in Cambridge, and he decided I was the right person for the job. When the department finally made up its mind a year later, the offer was delayed even further, while the University bureaucracy did its work. After weeks and weeks of further delay and confused phone calls with the chair, when the offer finally did come, it came without tenure, which was a shock. From my first phone call with the chair the year prior, the assumption was I would be hired with tenure. I had been teaching for eight years and had published a "big" book. Love it or hate it, it had made a splash. It was time for tenure.

Luckily, I had already received a tenured offer from UC Davis—500 miles to the north—without any difficulty at all, so I told the UCSD chair, as politely as I could, to shove it. It was the first time I had let my anger show in a professional setting, the first time I told someone off. After hanging up, I was equal parts horrified and exhilarated. The chair had tried to convince me that I'd earn tenure in short order without any problem. I replied with a line I've used ever since: Being tenured is like being pregnant; there is no such thing as "almost." I told him I would happily go to Davis.

The chair made a quick phone call to the authorities and called back a few minutes later and offered tenure. "It's a comedy, not a trage-dy," he said, trying to make light of what had just happened.

Although my negotiation, if one could call it that, was successful, I should have taken this as a sign of what the institution was like. They weren't quite sure I had the right stuff. I should have stepped back and thought about what was happening; at a minimum, we weren't starting off on the right foot. Even my rather orthodox new therapist in Boston (I had finally ditched the Buddhist) who rarely commented directly on what was happening in my life, startled me by saying, "I don't like the way they've treated you."

I didn't like it either.

But it was already early May. There was no time or energy to think carefully about anything. In just a few short weeks my job and salary at Harvard were ending, and I needed to know where I was headed. So as the crumbling Soviet Union struggled to contain the nuclear fallout at Chernobyl, I considered my options. The San Diego campus then had a better academic reputation than Davis, the city was much, much larger, and there was the ocean. The small town of Davis was isolated and hot in California's mostly agricultural central valley, and I tend to melt in hot weather.

San Diego it was.

I began looking for a place to live. I was drawn to the beach, and almost rented there, but I ended up choosing Hillcrest, the gayest and most urban neighborhood. I had a difficult time finding a place; every-thing was more expensive than I expected and money was tight, having just bought my first car. When I finally did sign a lease and move into a small one-bedroom apartment, for at least two months I didn't really unpack more than was absolutely necessary. I stumbled around, stub-bing my toes on unpacked boxes, fishing out clothes and books as I needed them. I stored my great grandmother's fine china tea set in the garage, where it was promptly stolen.

I had convinced myself, when considering the move from Harvard and Boston, that a big change was better than a small change, better California than Connecticut (Wesleyan had also looked me over). This was certainly a big change—huge—but I was no longer sure I knew what I was doing.

I was completely disoriented. The sun was too strong and the freeways were too fast. It never rained. Where was the subway? Where were the cabs? The bookstores? The deciduous trees? Neighborhoods one could walk around? Everyone, it seemed, was gorgeous, tan, and twenty-five. The gay men all had military haircuts (in fact, half seemed to really be in the Navy or Marine corps) and walked around shirtless, to show off their perfectly muscled bodies.

Everywhere, I overheard conversations about astrology and real estate, the yin and yang of California life. My colleagues talked openly about house prices and what I could afford (never once at Harvard did anyone discuss any aspect of money; gentlemen did not discuss such vulgar matters). "Actually, I was over at his house last night, and we had a good jacuzzi," one colleague said about another, after describing the house with the jacuzzi in considerable detail. I tried to picture two Harvard colleagues naked in a hot tub together—the mind reeled.

Where am I?

Moving from Beacon Hill and Harvard to Hillcrest and UCSD is about as far as one can go while staying in the same country, and I needed time to acclimate (and find a new wardrobe), but at the time that didn't occur to me. I felt like I had been dropped into the deep end of the pool without being taught how to swim. I was homesick. I was feeling desperate. I had made a terrible mistake. Although the ocean dazzled me and the weather was perpetually lovely, I had the sickening feeling that I didn't want to be there.

I fantasized about going back to Boston and driving a cab until I could figure out what to do with myself. I comforted myself with the notion that I wouldn't be the only educated cab driver in Boston. Once I had gotten into a cab and the driver was reading John Rawls. Maybe we could start a union, I mused, cab drivers with advanced degrees.

The feel of the UCSD campus only added to my dismay about where I had landed. Although the department eventually moved, twice, when I first arrived it was housed in buildings left over from World War II. They were dilapidated, dark, and depressing, and I had my first ever episode of *déjà vu*. There was a main building and an annex; I was stuck in the annex. It had been a temporary barracks or office, meant to be torn down at the end of the war, yet here it was, forty years later. It smelled musty, felt damp, lacked insulation, and there was no air conditioning. As the sun grew stronger over the course of the day, it grew stifling. The walls were painted what might have been, at one time, beige, but were now the color of grey mud. The furniture was cheap and falling apart. Bookshelves collapsed as I stocked them with my heavy law books.

And there was no escape. There was no place on campus to go for coffee or lunch; at the time, no student center, no faculty club. The library had no faculty carrels. The institution hadn't existed before 1960 and was still putting itself together. The campus was completely isolated from the surrounding neighborhoods. Parking was at a premium, so no one dared leave campus for lunch and risk losing a parking space. Everybody ate bag lunches. I bought a cardboard sandwich every day from a small convenience store near the office, the closest thing to a restaurant the campus provided at the time, apart from dorm cafeterias. The office and setting eerily reminded me of working on my dissertation, but this time I was 3,000 miles from Harvard Square.

To make matters worse, given my mood, everyone was perpetually cheerful. This was not the slightly arrogant, aloof disdain of all manner of things, softened by sardonic humor, that permeated Cambridge and Boston. Especially cheerful was Betsy, the department administrator, with whom I had many dealings while getting settled. Betsy was a permanently optimistic Christian Scientist who had run the department forever, and everyone deferred to her. She tolerated no complaints, no expressions of negativity whatsoever, about anything. One day I innocently mentioned how difficult it was to find a parking space near our offices. She was aghast, and her expression suggested I had just confessed to murdering children in a Satanic ritual. We clashed repeatedly over the smallest matters. A few days later she upbraided me for putting a note to another member of the staff in a department envelope, rather than just leaving it on the desk—shameful waste of an envelope. I learned to put on the largest smile I could manage when speaking to her and compliment her on her clothes (which were, in fact, lovely; she was paid more than most members of the faculty).

Slowly, some of my new colleagues began noticing my presence, and one or two invited me over for a meal. But this was a completely different social world than what I was used to, and for me not a comfortable one. Lunches with friendly peers or the one or two senior colleagues who were aware of my existence, the most common form of socializing in Cambridge, were out, since there was no place on the UCSD campus to eat. Everything here seemed to revolve around families and entertaining at home. Four members of the department had just had babies, including one faculty couple married to each other, and others had young children. Almost everyone seemed to be living rather stereotypical suburban lives in La Jolla or small towns to the north, rather than in the city of San Diego, which lay to the south, where I had planted myself.

Since I possessed neither house, spouse, cooking abilities, nor children, I did not really fit in. Had I been partnered—preferably to someone who cooked—things probably would have been easier. I would then have been just like everyone else but for one tiny little difference—a quasi-acceptance not unfamiliar in late twentieth century America, where, in many quarters—certainly among the educated and professional—domesticated, partnered homosexuality was increasingly acceptable. But as a *single* gay man in 1986, I was almost invisible.

One day soon after arriving I heard two colleagues talking as they slowly walked by my open office window. Professor A had been in the department a long time. Colleague B had, like me, just arrived. Professor A invited Colleague B and his wife over for a Sunday gathering of the department and other assorted university types. Professor A then asked Colleague B if he thought Colleague C, also newly arrived, would be comfortable coming, since he, Colleague C, was unmarried, and would be "the only single person there."

At that moment I finally understood the true meaning of the question "what am I, chopped liver?" Colleague C soon married.

At UCSD the hiring of a tenured, openly gay faculty member was rather big news around campus, it seemed. There weren't very many of us, given the size of the place, although more would arrive as time went on. Even people in remote departments and programs seemed to know I was gay before I met them—a member of the personnel committee (also chair of a department) had been telling people what was, apparently, big news. When meeting other people, there was often a brief but unmistakable pause in the conversation that would have been filled with discussion of one's spouse and children.

Miss Kate was beginning to feel like the character she played in *Woman of the Year*—a fish out of water, unfamiliar with normal, day-to-day life, such as the rules of baseball or how to cook a simple meal for Spencer Tracy.

I would have been deliriously happy to have found a partner, bought a house, gotten a dog or two, and invited my colleagues over for brunch. I almost did find Him—The One—but then the most likely candidate, a sweet and slightly dim San Diego native, came over one Friday evening and, instead of cooking dinner, as he usually did, told me he was giving up men for Jesus Christ.

"Well . . . at least you were playing in the major leagues," an East Coast friend helpfully pointed out. There were, in fact, lots of religious fanatics of various stripes in San Diego, as well as former members of cults. Many gay men attended a Sunday service of the "Science of Mind," a bizarre cousin of Christian Science.

Ironies abounded. Here I was, a nice Jewish boy, trying to settle down, thrown over for Jesus. And, more profoundly, no matter how deeply feminist or queer theorists criticize it, no matter how cogently it can be described as an anachronistic remnant of patriarchy, one model still dominates everyone's personal life, equally those who live it and those who don't—living in pairs, being half of a couple. In a culture where entertaining at home is the overwhelmingly preferred form of social life, the model dominates all the more.

Sex in the age of AIDS, of course, complicated the search for The One. As Dale Peck has written of the era, "sex would forever straddle the line between meaninglessness and metaphor."

There was a protocol among gay men about sex: If you have not had it by the end of the second date, or, at the latest, the end of the third, then it's only a matter of time until one of you will utter the three words Woody Allen says are the worst in the English language, "Let's be friends."

So one had to hurry. Except negotiating what needed to be discussed couldn't be hurried, and was sure to spoil the romance more quickly than an admission of a secret wife and six children in Omaha. More than one candidate to be The One exited as quickly as possible when I broached the subject of safe sex or HIV status.

I felt like I was trying to play Anne Baxter, the evil actress wannabe in *All About Eve*, facing a skeptical George Sanders, playing newspaper columnist Addison DeWitt.

"We sat and talked," Anne says about the married playwright she was trying to lure away from Celeste Holm, his wife, so that he would write wonderful plays in which she could star.

George is incredulous. "You sat and *talked*?"

"We sat and talked, Addison. I'm looking for a run of the play contract."

Only no one actually wanted to sit and talk. I was in a movie with only one character.

Gail Caldwell, a fine writer, describes her situation as a single woman in a way that captures mine as well: "A lot of my adult life," she says, "has been spent within shouting distance of others but in my own tent."

Not a bad way to live, I have discovered, over time, but harder to fit in. Tents in Southern California are expensive, so solo tents are rather tiny. Hard to invite the department over for a meal.

There is an advantage to having a separate tent, Caldwell also points out. Romantic partners and children always get first shot at being the main character, changing the plot around. For better or worse, after losing The One to Jesus in my mid-thirties, and having landed in this strange place, I suspected that the plot would be mine, all mine.

Altogether, I was more than ready to throw myself into teaching. I assumed the classroom, at least, would be familiar territory. But here, too, I had entered a different world. Classes were much larger than I was used to, and larger classes were not well suited to my teaching style, which was to lecture just a little and to ask questions to stimulate discussion of the material—close to the classic Socratic method of law schools, which was the best way to get students to consider the ins and outs of complex constitutional cases, to see all sides. And the student body was very different from the Ivy League—less well prepared, more used to lectures, not used to give and take.

At first, students couldn't even hear me. I did not have a strong enough voice to project to the back of the large classrooms and was forced to use a microphone. A student wearing a wetsuit would come from the AV office to hook me up the first few times; he surfed between assignments. I asked him if it was dangerous to handle electronic equipment while wet, but he seemed unconcerned. One day he was quite late. "The waves were great," he told me, dripping a bit and smiling.

Wired for sound, feeling a bit like a TV talk-show host, I would ask questions, the students would stare at me blankly, and I would feel a sense of panic rising in my stomach. After the first few experiences of this, I would go back to my office, put my head on my desk, and fall immediately to sleep, a sure sign that I was in trouble and did not know what to do.

The cab-driving fantasy seemed more and more attractive.

Slowly I learned to lecture more in every class, learned that I needed to explain my methods and my expectations, and to make reading assignments shorter. I also learned to appreciate the different circumstances from which the student body came. These were not the sons and daughters of privilege, but, often, first generation college students working twenty to thirty hours each week to support themselves and pay for college.

Few of them found their way to my office, but from those who did I began to understand the different world into which I had been plunged. A young woman of color was the first undergraduate to come to see me. She was trembling with nervousness—at an institution of this size, undergraduate students did not have all that much direct contact with faculty. I tried to put her at ease, and slowly, over time, she told me her story. Her father was a police officer in LA, and she wanted more than anything to go to law school. She was working eighteen hours each week doing paperwork in a car rental agency. No one in her family had ever been to college. She knew very little about what she would need to do to get into a law school, or how she would pay for it. I explained the process and told her she would be an attractive candidate and could well be given financial aid. Her nervousness gradually ebbed, she came back to see me a number of times, and I thought for the first time about the ways in which issues of class shaped higher education, but were never discussed, at least not at elite institutions—and thinking of itself as an elite institution was, accurately or not, a central component of UCSD's self-image. We do what we do, take it or leave it—that was the reigning ethos. The trickle-down theory of teaching.

During the spring quarter of my first year I experienced my first total academic disaster. I was asked to teach Ethics, a required course for freshmen in one of UCSD's colleges (the university is divided into several different undergraduate colleges, each with different general education requirements). This time the size of the class was overwhelming—nearly two hundred in a large amphitheater. The week before the start of the class, feverishly writing lectures late into the night, I got little sleep, and on the morning of the first lecture managed to cut my head on a kitchen cabinet and had to go to an emergency room just before the first class. As I arrived at the lectern my shirt was splattered with blood and I was doped up on painkillers.

My lectures did not go well from the start. I pitched way too high and the students were lost; many simply tuned out. They talked while I lectured, read the newspaper, frowned at me. One young woman would bring polish and do her nails. Writing the lectures was torture. The topic didn't seem to me to lend itself to lectures at all. Ethics was a topic that seemed to require back and forth, nuance, careful probing. I worked like crazy writing lectures that fell completely flat.

As at Harvard I tried talking to my colleagues about classroom issues, and got the same reaction. "Don't sweat it, teaching counts for nothing here," a senior administrator told me without a hint of embarrassment.

Over time I learned the UC way. Undergraduates had dollar signs on their backs—the legislature funded the university on a per-pupil basis. The incentives were therefore to make classes as large as possible. The priorities for the use of the funds were to support graduate education and research, which is what everyone really cared about; undergraduate teaching was a necessary evil. Some might be good at it but it didn't matter; most were indifferent, which didn't matter either. In my fourteen years there, I very seldom heard the department seriously discuss teaching ability or the needs of the undergraduate curriculum when making a hiring or promotion decision—and we eventually had close to 1,000 majors, almost as large as the student bodies at the smaller liberal arts colleges.

I was miserable, so miserable at first that I wanted out. So at the end of my first year I started to look around for other jobs, and applied for a job as a dean at Bard College, a small college in upstate New York.

Their job ad was ambiguous. It wasn't clear what kind of dean this would be, but such was my state of mind that I didn't care. They called right away ... they were interested ... very interested, it seemed.

"We're looking to get married, we're not looking to go out," the college president said to me over the phone. They flew me out right away.

Everything that could possibly go wrong on that trip did. My non-stop flight from San Diego to New York had to make an emergency landing, so we sat on the tarmac in Phoenix without air conditioning for three hours. Arriving limp at JFK, where I was supposed to pick up a car, I found that the rental car company had given away my car because I was four hours late. After much delay, they located a huge, luxury sedan for me, which I knew I'd have trouble driving. There was torrential rain as I made my way up the Hudson Valley, and sure enough I lost control of the car at one point and ended up in a ditch. I finally arrived at Bard around midnight, where they had said they would have accommodation for me, which turned out to be a stifling, airless attic room in a dorm. Their school year had ended and the place was deserted. The interview began at 8:00 a.m. the next morning, but there was nowhere to have breakfast, nor did they offer any. I had slept little, eaten no dinner, and was completely rattled. Lunch was with a group of staff members who fired constant questions at me, and so I didn't have a chance to eat more than a few bites. I've never been so hungry in my life.

Somehow I got through the day, but it became clear that this position was on the student life side of the college, not the curricular or academic, and I had no real experience in student life jobs. The whole, jinxed trip felt like a waste of time.

Except for one thing. They had me meet with a group of students, and I was completely charmed by them. They were smart, funny, engaged. They asked interesting questions—far more interesting than the questions asked by the staff—and cared deeply about the college and their education.

A seed was planted.

Back in San Diego for the summer, I began looking around for things to do in the community outside the university. I got involved with the local ACLU and with an LGBT community theatre company that was just getting off the ground. Eventually, I would join the board of directors of both groups, and the theatre, especially, gave me a sense of connection I did not feel on campus.

I loved the energy in and around the theatre. We chose a play, we rehearsed the play, we performed the play. It was intense for a few brief months, and then it was over, a success or not, but, either way, on to the next one. No time for angst. More often than not our shows were well received, even though we performed them for many years in make-shift spaces that the local newspaper once said had all the charm of a welfare office. And the theatre gave me contact with the gay community, which I craved. In those early years the members of the board did everything from running the box office to building scenery to selling drinks at intermission. We became quite successful, and I eventually served as president of the board. We were a fixture on the local arts scene.

As the next fall quarter began at UCSD, I was determined to do what I could to take control of my teaching. To the consternation of my colleagues I refused to teach Ethics again. That subject should not be taught to first year students in that format, I argued, pointing to my low student evaluations. And I began limiting enrollment in my other courses to seventy-five, which was still larger than optimal but was more manageable. With seventy-five I could manage at least some back and forth with the students. My colleagues weren't happy with that, either, but little by little I learned how to make those classes enjoyable, both for me and for the students. Tenure had to be good for something, I thought to myself as I argued with my colleagues about class size, and held firm.

For the first time in my life, I was saying no to what was expected of me. It would at times get me in trouble, in later years, these occasions of saying no, but this time, at least, the trouble passed rather quickly, largely because no one at UCSD really cared who did or did not teach what.

The classroom improved that second year at UCSD, and I was beginning to feel somewhat reconciled to where I was, when I faced my first merit review, a form of torture first used for horse thieves in Elizabethan England, somehow transplanted to sunny, modern-day California. The procedure controls the professional lives of the 18,000 faculty members in the University system and is worth discussing in some detail, since it represents, in extreme form, much of what is currently wrong in American academia.

Every other year (for assistant and associate professors), or every three years (for full professors), faculty members are required to undergo a formal review, during which they present their newly published scholarship or, supposedly, their work in progress. Each rank had a series of steps: Associate Professor Step 1, Step 2, Step 3, and so forth—which is highly unusual in academia. Most institutions have three ranks—assistant, associate, and full professor, and perhaps a fourth—distinguished professor. But at the University of California, the ranks are further subdivided, making the system resemble something akin to the army. If one's scholarly progress at UC is deemed sufficient, one is promoted to the next step, which includes a modest (or, further along, not so modest) increase in salary.

The review is formal, and public. One presents one's work first to one's departmental colleagues. In political science, the candidate was asked to submit a "sliced bread" memo (explain why you're the greatest thing since sliced bread). On the basis of that, the chair would prepare a memo that circulated among colleagues for discussion and then, under the procedures in place at the time, that memo would be sent first to the divisional dean, and then to the Star Chamber (officially labeled the Committee on Academic Personnel—CAP), consisting of university worthies, who would pass judgment. Their evaluation would be reported to the Lord Chancellor (official title, the Senior Vice Chancellor for Academic Affairs) who would have the final say.

In essence, each member of the faculty underwent the equivalent of a mini tenure review every other year (or every three years). "It's like running for Congress," a new colleague said to me—a perpetual campaign.

In theory, the system makes sense. Salaries are (supposedly) on a public scale and pegged to concrete achievement as judged by one's peers, not the whims of one person, a department chair or a dean. There are multiple levels of review—checks and balances applied to academia. The same standards are applied throughout the University, professors of English and professors of Engineering subject to the same process.

During my first merit review, I had one new article accepted by a very good journal—the top journal in its field, actually—so I thought there would be no problem, especially since I had just arrived. I was, in many ways, still unpacking, still disoriented, still figuring out how to teach UCSD undergraduates.

Then one day, returning to my office from a class that had gone well, in a wonderful mood, I found a note on my door from the chair: "I need to see you."

The good mood evaporated immediately, and there was a sinking feeling in my stomach.

"There's a problem with your file. CAP has turned down your merit increase," the chair said solemnly. We had the right to appeal.

I asked why they had turned me down. After hemming and hawing and waxing poetic about the mysteries of life and of the University—the two seemingly conflated—he told me one article was not "sufficient." When I asked why not, especially since the article had appeared in a leading journal, the chair had very little to say beyond pointing out the small number of pages the article occupied in the journal.

"So if it were a few pages longer, it would have been ok?"

"Well. . . ." More poetry about the mysteries of life, mostly irrelevant, but the underlying message was clear: I wasn't working hard enough. These should be the most productive years of my career, he said. I was falling behind. Produce more pages; publish, publish, publish.

I was aghast—is it really possible they count pages, I wondered? It seemed ridiculous, anti-intellectual. I thought for a moment the chair was trying to be funny.

He wasn't.

"How many pages are required?" I asked. It seemed like the obvious follow-up question.

"It's not that simple, there's no formula," he replied.

"There's no formula, but this number of pages isn't sufficient?"

Round and round we went. The fiction of Kafka, read in high school, made a sudden reappearance in my brain.

I walked out of the chair's office, got in my car and drove to one of the minor buildings of the Scripps Institute of Oceanography, the unit around which the entire campus had been built. The small, all-but-abandoned wood building was on a cliff, with a balcony overlooking the beach and the perfect blue ocean below, and the little building—a shack, really—was always deserted. There was a bench on the balcony, and in the next few years I would often go there when things got bumpy.

I looked down at a group of young men playing volleyball. Probably graduate students, oceanographers, I thought. I wonder if they had been told the secret formula, the right number of pages.

In my various talks with the chair, he never mentioned his opinion of the article. We discussed only numbers—number of pages, number of chapters of forthcoming book completed, how many might be published separately, and so forth. Not long ago, I found a reference to that first California article as "often cited," and was startled out of my wits, since what I remembered was that the article was judged to be inconsequential.

Given the reigning ethos and my recently accepted article, I committed another sin. I made the mistake of saying that perhaps the material with which I was working was better suited to a series of such articles, as opposed to a book. That seemed to be what they wanted.

That brought even more commotion, since I had previously reported the material would go into a book.

A very senior department colleague called Peter Irons on the carpet. "Harry needs to know that I spent a good bit of my own political capital getting him hired, and he needs to provide the book he promised," he declared. What kind of "capital" was involved was left unclear. Delivering this message to Peter, rather than to me, was, of course, yet another way of making me feel like a supplicant. Once again, I wondered if I were chopped liver—which was beginning to seem like a recurring theme. CAP was also not happy with the possible replacement of a book by a series of articles—although they were also not happy that there weren't more articles.

Through all this drama, the content of my work—what I had to say—was never once discussed, or even mentioned, in the back and forth between me and the chair, the chair and CAP, or Very Senior Colleague and Peter. Were my ideas good ideas or not? Was I onto something worthwhile in that article, short though it might be? No one seemed to have anything to say about that.

In this and my other encounters with the UC merit system, a profound sense of alienation began to shape how I felt about contemporary university life, at least this West Coast, public version. I realized slowly that I no longer could be Miss Kate at the beginning of *Stage Door*—an innocent in the ways of the world upon whom fortune had smiled. I needed somehow to turn myself into Hepburn at the end of the movie, a savvy career woman who knows how the world works and does whatever needs to be done. (Of course in that movie Kate's success triggered the suicide of a competitor, but maybe that wouldn't be necessary.)

I looked around for comrades, allies, friends. For a while after I arrived, I was friendly with two gay men in the social sciences. We'd have the occasional meal together, but the two of them would chatter on endlessly about the latest University gossip, who was up and who was down, who got promoted and who didn't, who published what where. Both were true believers in UCSD's destiny as a great university rivaling Berkeley, UCLA, Stanford, even Harvard . . . that is, if UCSD would get tougher, eliminate the academic proletariat. I would mostly listen, occasionally asking a question.

I remember in particular a few Sunday brunches at the Big Kitchen, a homey San Diego lunchroom where Whoopi Goldberg had once worked as a waitress before she became famous. I tried every tactic I could think of to steer the conversation away from the University, from who was up and who was down.

Tell me more about this place.

Gorgeous weather, isn't it?

I'm getting tickets for the ballet, want to come?

Isn't that guy over there gorgeous?

Have either of you ever tried surfing?

No non-University topic worked for more than sixty seconds. The friendships didn't last.

Over the years, as I came to various conclusions about the UC system and the behavior it encouraged, its flaws were impossible to gloss over, and my sense of alienation deepened. On campus I often felt disoriented, out of place, jet-lagged without the travel. I spent more time at the theatre, with the ACLU, more time driving around San Diego's far-flung outer reaches, looking at model homes I couldn't afford.

Each time I faced an unusually difficult day at UCSD, one on which the mismatch between the university and me was again made glaringly apparent, I made haste for the ocean. Sometimes the Scripps beach near campus, sometimes Coronado, where another volleyball game played by impossibly blonde, young, perfect male bodies never seemed to end.

"Where do these guys come from?" I asked a friend. "Central casting," he replied.

In one direction on Coronado one gazed at Point Loma, a dramatic and lovely cliff. In the other direction stood the Hotel Del, a proud and still functioning wooden structure where Presidents had stayed and Marilyn Monroe and Jack Lemmon had cavorted in *Some Like It Hot*. Off beyond the hotel, in the far distance when the sun burned through the haze, one could see the hills of Mexico.

The smell and sound of the surf, the perfect sunshine moderated by the cool breeze, the thermostat permanently stuck at seventy-two degrees, had a calming effect on me like almost nothing else, an effect a sardonic friend assured me was better than antidepressants.

And then, inevitably, reality would return.

Like many who chafe at a bureaucratic system, especially one that claims to be democratic, I initially thought my unhappiness was my fault, and I felt like a failure. Only gradually did I come to realize that my shortcomings, real as they might be, were not the whole story.

Perhaps the biggest flaw in the UC system, and one I felt profoundly from the beginning, is that teaching counts for absolutely nothing. Publication is the only thing that matters, lip service by the University to the contrary notwithstanding. Spend a summer developing a new course? Unimportant, not rewarded. Not even worth discussing. Spend a quarter or two rewriting lectures for an existing course? Forget it.

Needless to say, this disdain for the importance of teaching has a huge impact on how people spend their time and on the quality of what transpires in the classroom. University faculties are composed of smart people with PhDs who can figure out what gets rewarded and what does not. Undergraduate teaching does not; in fact, it hardly registers at all. The losers in the system, then, are students, who are paying, or whose parents are paying the bills, if not through ever-rising tuition, then through tax dollars, to the tune of $2 billion each year in California.

To paraphrase the late Illinois Senator Everett Dirkson, a billion here, a billion there, pretty soon it's real money.

No doubt, the people of California give the University so much money because they think it will be spent educating their children, future citizens of the state. But undergraduates are way, way down the list of what the University cares about. It is not an accident that the student rebellion of the Sixties began at Berkeley, where, in the prescient words of Mario Savio, the leader of the Free Speech Movement, the undergraduate student was becoming the "new dispossessed." And it's not at all surprising that contemporary public support for higher education is lukewarm at best, and that criticism of its performance from all quarters is rapidly increasing, when the priorities of many universities are so out of whack and the experience of so many undergraduates in the classroom is mediocre at best, all while cost rapidly escalates.

But even if one accepts the University's priorities, there is still the all-important question of what counts, of how scholarship is defined and evaluated. CAP consists of representatives from many different fields and schools, and, at UCSD, the medical school and the sciences dominate. Given the degree of specialization in academia today, no one—in any field—has the expertise to judge the actual content of articles, papers, and books written in fields far beyond their own. How is a Professor of Medicine, a cardiologist, supposed to judge a book on T.S. Elliot's poetry, or a paper on the inner workings of state legislatures? She can't. It's preposterous to think that she could. What matters instead is the documentable, provable judgment of peers in each field.

At most institutions, the relevant peers are your department colleagues, perhaps with the opinion of a divisional dean added in, and personnel committees and administrators rely almost entirely on their judgment for routine salary bumps. Formal outside evaluation, elsewhere on the planet, is usually required only for major milestones—tenure, promotion to full professor, promotion to an endowed chair. At those milestones, most institutions invoke peer review by writing to scholars in the given field, asking for an evaluation of the candidate's full body of work. Publishing in peer-reviewed venues—certain journals, university presses—is expected, where appropriate to the subject, but the outside letters are usually important no matter where the work has appeared. If the outside letters and the department's judgment do not match up, the case becomes a difficult case.

But at UC, perhaps because every aspect of the system is so large, unwieldy, and bureaucratized—from the budget to the admissions process—departments aren't fully trusted to evaluate their own members, and so documentable outside judgment becomes the default requirement for every review.

The only way to document outside approval for every step, every modest salary increase, is to require a constant stream of new, peer-reviewed publications. In essence, UC takes academia's requirement of outside peer approval, usually applied only a few times during a career, and makes it perpetual. Instead of being expected to produce a body of work over a reasonable period of time, UC faculty are expected to produce new publications every two or three years, and the only publications that really matter are the ones published in peer reviewed venues. Peer review at UC is the catechism, the Eucharist, and the holy grail rolled into one, and my colleagues were true believers, rigorously applying the University's gospel. During each review, one was required to turn in a "biobib," including a list of publications, with a bright line (literally) drawn between new publications and old. Everything depends on how much is listed above the line.

As in most religious systems, repetition and the threat of excommunication is required to sustain the ideology. But also like most religious beliefs, if one looks closely, there are cracks and contradictions.

As I developed my critique of the system over the years, I couldn't quite decide if I was the other Hepburn—Audrey—in *The Nun's Story*, sharing the church's basic values but chafing at the most restrictive rules, or if I was Audrey in *Breakfast at Tiffany's*, a half-crazy misfit (but still lovable). Perhaps I was Linda Blair in *The Exorcist*, a case of simple possession.

The most serious problem with the system from my perspective was that if peer review is the necessary proof of scholarly worthiness, then work in progress, not yet publishable or published, drops out of the picture—for example, a paper presented at a conference but not yet published. That means that the system is biased in favor of those scholars whose work is churned out in small, bite-sized pieces rather than in more lengthy formats. It also favors those fields that have available many peer review journals over those which do not, which is a matter of economics.

When I first published an article in a law review, I was told, by a colleague in another department who had served on CAP, that it counts as much as half of a normal article. Why, I inquired (ignoring the use of the word "normal")? Because law reviews are not anonymously peer reviewed, I was solemnly told. This is true—law reviews are edited in-house, by faculty and law students, and they usually do not send articles out to scholars in the field for anonymous assessment. But law reviews are an appropriate venue for my field, I pointed out, trying hard to keep my temper. "So in other words," I said, "you are telling me that if I continue publishing in law reviews, my salary will suffer."

He nodded yes and shrugged.

Then there is the problem of the book.

At a conference a few years after arriving, I ran into a colleague who had recently joined another UC department. "How's the book coming?" I asked.

"I've dropped it," he said, with a pained look on his face. We were standing in the crowded lobby of the conference hotel, and we moved to the edge for a little privacy.

"Why? What happened?" I was more than surprised—we had talked about his book project, it sounded terrific, and he was excited about it. I felt panic as I imagined an illness or Act of God.

"It will take too long. I need to be writing articles."

I didn't know what to say—he was right. If he took a long time writing a book, his status and salary would suffer. He had made a rational decision.

His decision was rational, but the system that forced it upon him is out of whack. For it can take a long time to write a good book, sometimes a very long time. Some books may have chapters that can be published along the way; some may not. For one thing, publishers often do not like to publish books if too many of the chapters have previously appeared in print, and for another, some books may present sustained or intricate arguments, the pieces of which do not make much sense in isolation.

Years after arriving, a colleague, an Associate Professor, was up for his first post-tenure review. He had just been awarded tenure on the basis of a long, truly original book. Roughly fifteen months later— because that's how the system works—he faced his next merit review. He was, not surprisingly, only in the planning stages of a new, complex book project, and showed us a précis, a plan of action. He had no new publications. The department argued to CAP that he was doing exactly what he should be doing and doing it well, embarking on a new, important research project that would take some time.

Not only was he not awarded a step increase, but the letter from the Vice Chancellor contained the following priceless advice: Perhaps you should move Professor X to the Lecturer series (Lecturer being a second-class status at an institution like UCSD), since he seems uninterested in scholarship. Professor X was so upset by this that I suggested professional counseling. In another case, an Associate Professor was denied a step despite the fact that he was doing a great deal of original archival research, requiring travel abroad, for a new book. When we protested the denial (I was chair at the time, so wrote the letter), the Vice Chancellor informed me—through a dean, of course, making it impossible to respond—that my letter of protest was "inappropriate."

I work at a factory,

I wrote in my journal during that incident,

and all that matters is the number of units produced per quarter. No questions allowed.

As a result of all this, not surprisingly, many people skew their choices about how to spend their scholarly time. Reliability (in the sense of work likely to be published in certain forms and in certain venues) becomes more important than originality or creativity. When I chaired the department, I heard several colleagues—distinguished scholars all, some of them major figures in their fields—say, in so many words, "well, what I'd like to work on is X, but since I'm up for a merit review this year/next year/in two years, I'm going to do Y instead." A university should want tenured scholars to work on X, not Y. The system also encourages repetition. Developing a data set and mining it for article after article, or developing an argument and then tweaking it ever so slightly, becomes, in this system, rational behavior.

During my first merit review, barely a year after arriving, I was pushing forward with a project that existed in various pieces, some chapters of which had been published, others of which had been conference papers. It was going slowly, to be sure. The job market, seeing if there was what some called LAH (Life After Harvard), took time and energy. But by the time I got to that first merit review in California, I could see that I was also in the middle of a perfectly normal, and useful, scholarly process—figuring out what I had to say, how original it was or wasn't, whether I could support my point of view, whether it should be a book or a series of articles—that is, a standard scholarly muddle.

My muddle served me well, I can say in retrospect. The book I eventually published, after six years at UC and several difficult merit reviews, is a lot better than it would have been had I rushed it into print. The book garnered its own panel at the APSA when it appeared— relatively unusual—and a later scholar described my work in his own book as "path-breaking" and "remarkably bold" in its challenge to "the dominant view in the discipline" of its subject, constitutional argument (God bless him).

I have no doubt that the book would not have been as good if I had published it on UC's schedule, rather than on my own timeline. Originality isn't quick or easy in a field as well trod as constitutional law. Walter Murphy, my mentor at Princeton—who was on everybody's "A" list of scholars before he died—took close to twenty years to publish a similar book. These kinds of books don't contain empirical observations or *data*. Data sets are wonderful, but not every area of scholarship has them, and a university geared toward those who do is favoring but one segment of academia, promoting only one form of knowledge.

But there are even deeper problems with the system, I eventually came to see. It turns knowledge into a commodity, a quantifiable, verifiable commodity, and it operates on the assumption that all scholarly commodities can and should be produced at the same pace, in the same manner, by every one of the thousands of faculty members at the University of California. A Shakespeare specialist and an engineer who studies earthquakes, a classicist working on a translation and a mathematician developing formal models of disease transmission, should all be producing peer-reviewed publications at a steady clip, should all, at every stage of their career, produce new publications that can be listed above the line in Section A of their biobib. Mastering a body of knowledge, keeping up in one's field, and skillfully, creatively transmitting that knowledge to students—what used to be the essence of a university—doesn't count for much. And for faculty, there is no room for experimentation or self-development. If you want to study a new subfield, learn a new language to do research about another country, learn a new skill, or, God forbid, spend time on your teaching, your salary and status will suffer. The system assumes you arrive at the University fully formed as a scholar, an expert on X, Y, or Z, ready to churn out a particular kind of publication for the next forty years.

The crucial word in that sentence is *or*. Having interests in X *and* Y *and* Z can be a problem; broad interests can be a detriment. I began my academic career with in interest in two subfields, constitutional law and political psychology, and wrote a dissertation putting them together. Already, that was a bit of a mistake; I "should" have chosen one or the other and stuck to it. Instead, along the way, I did the opposite, adding interests in political theory and gender and sexuality. I've made scholarly contributions, some substantial, some more modest, in all of these subfields, but spreading out in such a manner does not fit the UC mold. At Harvard, when I arrived I was classified as an Americanist; by the time I left, I was representing political theory on the department's committee of senior honors examiners. I considered that an achievement. Many—certainly at UC—would call it a mistake, a sign that I wasn't a serious scholar.

The UC model further assumes that "scholarship" has only one meaning: publication. But scholarship has many meanings. Like most, I have spent a fair amount of time over the years serving as a discussant on panels at professional conferences. I have also reviewed manuscripts for journals and university and trade publishers. I have been asked to serve as an outside reviewer in tenure cases, during which the institution in question sends you a pile of the candidate's work to read, which is often quite a large pile of paper. All of these things take time, and require expertise. All of this is *scholarship*, and important, but it isn't publication. The two are not synonymous. If a major university asks me for a letter evaluating the scholarship of their incoming president so that he could be appointed to the faculty, as one did, and I take several weeks to read all his work and write a careful letter, that work counts for nothing.

At UC, all of this kind of activity—on which the profession depends—can be discussed under the heading of "service," which matters not at all. If it's not above the line in section A (publications) of one's biobib, it doesn't exist.

Together with these kinds of issues, in the digital age scholarship is evolving in a way that makes "peer review" a complex matter. I have, at times, participated in online professional discussions, and my sense is that the opinions and interpretations I've expressed there have received far more attention from scholars in the field than the average journal article, but there's no way to list such an entry on UC's biobib.

There is, moreover, a severe methodological bias in all of this. The system assumes that every scholar in every field is engaged in what scientists call discovery research: new data, new experiments, new information.

It's not in any way an accident that many large universities take as their model a particular type of scientific research. Since the creation of American research universities on the German model in the late nineteenth century, their main goal has been understood to be the creation of new knowledge—a definition that fits the sciences perfectly, but that fits other fields only to a degree. More to the point, post–World War II, federal research grants began providing prestigious universities with an astounding bounty of funds for scientific (and, in the Cold War, politically useful) work, which, especially at UC, the institution has come to rely upon—not just for departments where the funds are used directly, but also for the rest of the campus. Every federal research grant is taxed by the central administration (in academic parlance, grants are charged "overhead") and those funds—many millions every year—are used all over campus. In fact, those funds provide campus administrators one of their only real sources of discretionary income. It's not surprising, then, that the model of scientific research that relies on federal dollars dominates the modern research university.

To be sure, the University of California has a long, venerable history and an admirable goal—a high quality, public, multi-campus university, serving every part of a vast state, accessible, at least in theory, to millions of citizens over time. This is a profoundly democratic vision—higher education on a mass scale, in a state with a huge population and an economy rivaling that of many nations—by some measures, the seventh or eighth largest economy in the world. And UCSD, in particular, is a campus built around, dominated by, the sciences, with Scripps and the medical school bringing in an extraordinary amount of federal money. It was also a young, extremely ambitious campus, and, in the words of one observer, went from zero to sixty in five seconds.

It is perhaps unrealistic to expect any degree of nuance under these conditions. Huge institutions do not lend themselves to treating their employees as individuals, and a campus like UCSD, wanting to put itself on the map in record time, is not likely to equally value those who spend their time reading novels or Supreme Court cases and those who work on cancer or measure ocean warming.

Because scientific research is not only the most lucrative but also the easiest to track and count and justify to the bill-paying public, it is the standard against which everything is measured, not just at UCSD but throughout the gigantic system. The officially published history of UC boasts mostly of its "world renown for scientific achievement," and, when it comes to speaking about the modern period, after 1970, and "new intellectual horizons," singles out the creator of a new telescope for several paragraphs. One would never know, for example, that two extraordinarily important philosophers, Jacques Derrida and Herbert Marcuse, also taught at UC in the same era. The official history makes it clear: Science is in the driver's seat.

But the model of scientific research doesn't fit a great many scholarly fields, including most of the humanities, political theory, and a good bit of law. Heresy though it may be to say this, there is only so much to say about Shakespeare or Aristotle, or the Equal Protection Clause. So, in some disciplines and subfields within disciplines, much of what there is to say has been said already, and most new work on these kinds of subjects isn't very new at all.

On the other hand, absorbing, mastering, and teaching what has come before—which for ages was the essence of the humanities, and the more humanistic social sciences—is also a form of scholarship, and it doesn't take place only in graduate school. In the words of one prominent humanist, in some fields the task is rearticulation, not discovery.

When I pick up a new book or begin reading a new article about constitutional law, usually I know where the author is going after reading the first chapter or even a few pages; it's mostly been said before, again and again. There might be a slightly new spin, but the intellectual framework, the argument, at base, will be a rerun. My shelves are full of books written not because the author really had something new to say, but because the author needed a job, needed to earn tenure, needed to be promoted to full professor. Not many of these books are really original, and very few of them will stand the test of time. Many of them are no longer read.

This is not in any way the authors' fault; there are only so many ways to cook an egg. In a sense, scholars in some fields are trapped in a system that demands from them the nearly impossible—discovery, originality—as the price of routine advancement. The result is a mountain of paper containing endlessly repeated arguments and debates, often expressed in arcane and obscure language meant to look original and mask the fact that there is very little new being said. It's not coincidental that some subfields and scholars in the humanities have developed a convoluted vocabulary that only initiates can understand. Novelty, originality, is what the system demands. It has to come somewhere, in one form or another.

And there's more. When the task is interpretation and commentary, rather than experiments or data-gathering, there's another factor at play: Every argument is flawed, in one way or another—including, emphatically, your own. In graduate training, the ability to root out the flaws, the development of that critical faculty, is the name of the game—and therefore almost impossible not to apply to oneself. So not only is the path well-traveled; it leads, more often than not, to a position easy to challenge, to poke full of holes. On some level you are spending a great deal of time and energy chasing a chimera. There *is* no "truth," or "new" knowledge.

Realizing this can be paralyzing, especially in the early stages of a project. In the early weeks, months, even years of working on my second book, I would read over what I had written and get a sinking feeling in my stomach. I would toil away diligently and at length, the words would come, and then I would read over a draft and think:

Yes, but.

There is always a counter-argument. And, even more unsettling, it becomes painfully obvious that your argument flows directly from your premises, which are, in some ultimate sense, arbitrary. Different people would, could, did, use different premises to arrive at opposite conclusions.

Yes, but.

So you double down. You make your premises clear and defensible. But they are just that—premises. Theories. They may reflect or interpret reality, as best you see it, and the target of your theorizing may be vitally important, but your theory is not, in any fundamental sense, real. A defense of judicial activism or judicial restraint, no matter how learned and sophisticated, no matter what specific area of the law is being discussed, remains in the end a theory, an ideological stance. It can never be proven, and chances are there will be very few who start from different premises who will accept what you say.

But you keep at it—you are a scholar, after all, this is what you are supposed to be doing. You do your best to anticipate and answer the criticisms that you know could be, almost certainly will be, made, and the argument gets a little stronger. Yet after a while, after torturing yourself and making your argument as strong as you can, the whole enterprise begins to feel a bit like that weird film by Orson Welles starring Rita Hayworth—a house of mirrors. Look left, there's a gun pointed at you. Look right, it disappears.

Miss Kate always had trouble with roles like that; they made her head spin. She sometimes felt disoriented and was tempted to walk off the set. She needed take after take to get each scene right, and she was never really happy with her performance. The film's director always grew impatient.

I can't believe I've spent three years on this stuff,

I wrote in my journal in 1985, at a particularly low moment, when the argument wasn't gelling and I had only months to go on my Harvard contract. If it had been finished at that point, I would have been way ahead; in fact it took years more to come up with something I was willing to publish. And, comparatively speaking, it isn't just "stuff"; judged by the standards of the discipline and genre, it's pretty good. Maybe even very good. But for almost every one of those ten years, at least half the time, I wondered, on some nagging level, why adults actually spent time doing this kind of work.

I discovered quickly that saying "I'm working on a theory" didn't get me very far during UCSD merit reviews. And I also I discovered quickly that how one was treated at UCSD depended on how one fared during those reviews. At Harvard, faculty were mostly given the benefit of the doubt—assumed to be solid professionals who knew what they were doing, could make wise choices about how to spend their time. Working on a new book? Fine. It's taking a while? Sometimes it does. There and at Princeton what really seemed to matter was how well you knew your subject. At UC, all that mattered was what could be tallied up, counted, and verified on a regular schedule. There had been a number of senior faculty members at Harvard and Princeton who did not publish many articles, who took long stretches of time to write books, who would have had problems in the UC merit system.

At UCSD what mattered was where your next article—which better come soon—was going to be published, how much grant money you brought in, how many citations to your work could be found in the Social Science Citation Index. Never once in twelve years at Princeton and Harvard did I hear that Index mentioned, but I heard it mentioned six times in my first few months at UCSD (out of a combination of amusement and dismay, I kept track). I vividly remember one senior colleague, soon after I arrived, sending around a memo arguing against tenure for an assistant professor, prominently discussing the absence of citations in that Index. That this junior colleague's work (presented in a long book) might be cited in other books rather than journals, or might be valuable despite a small number of citations, did not enter the calculus.

After more than a decade of Ivy League gentility, I found it all distasteful to the point of near-despair. This was not academia as I had known it. No one seemed interested in my ideas. Only my numbers mattered.

The science bias of the UCSD campus was of a piece with the fact that most of my departmental colleagues fervently believed that our discipline would be, could be, was in fact a "science." A typical exchange with one of my colleagues went something like this. Seeking me out to discuss a question I had submitted for the written general exam for graduate students in American politics, he said my question was "okay, but there really ought to be a question that resembles political SCIENCE." I had submitted a question about the nature of judicial power, asking for illustrations from case law.

The question couldn't be answered with numbers or formal models; cases aren't amenable to scientific analysis. For one thing, some cases are important, others are not, so counting them, or counting votes on the Supreme Court, doesn't tell you a whole lot beyond the obvious. Analyzing cases for their content *does* make sense, but it's not science. A single case can affect millions of people or reshape the political process or determine the course of history.

I explained this, as best I could, to my skeptical colleague, and left my question as it was. But the exchange stuck with me. And then the school year was over ... and it was time to prepare my materials for another merit review.

During the summer before a merit review approached in the fall, a sense of dread would slowly take over. At times I was distracted, at times hyper-alert. Sleep eluded me. Small ailments would crop up, vague stomach problems or worsening allergies. I considered tranquilizers. I would feel like I was playing Kate in *Mary of Scotland*, one of her earliest films. The executioner's ax was approaching, and nothing, nothing, nothing could stop it. Kate was out of her depth.

Certainly all was not gloom and doom at UCSD; there were many experiences there I enjoyed and from which I benefitted. Occasional undergraduate honors students, with whom one worked closely. A summer seminar each year for Latin American academics and journalists, organized by my colleague Wayne Cornelius, where some of us were brought in to teach the visitors about various aspects of American politics—the men and women who attended were fascinating people, who often had insightful things to say about the US. Working with two colleagues in other departments on a course on Justice for first year students in one of UCSD's undergraduate colleges. Smart colleagues in all disciplines all over the place, some of whom became good friends.

And, to be fair to UC, along with certain kinds of research, it does one thing exceedingly well across the board—graduate education.

One day in the early Nineties there was a knock at my door, and a young looking man in paisley shorts and a torn T-shirt walked in. How unusual, I thought—an undergraduate, and it isn't even office hours. It must be some kind of emergency.

He introduced himself, and it turned out he wasn't an undergraduate, and there was no emergency. His name was Keith Bybee, and he wondered if we could do a graduate reading course in the next semester. We did. And little by little, Keith and I began to work together, and I became his advisor and the first reader of his dissertation. He was stunningly brilliant, and, at the same time, had his feet firmly planted on the ground. When he went out on the job market, Harvard's junior slot in our field was open and I recommended him for it.

He was quickly offered the job. I'm not sure which one of us was more surprised and pleased. Like me, like most, he did not earn tenure there; he moved on to an endowed chair at Syracuse University. But the fact that Harvard trusted my judgment sufficiently to hire my student felt like an affirmation, even a bit of vindication in some weird cosmic manner. They hired my student, not a Princeton or Yale PhD. It felt good, and for the first time I understood why some of my colleagues were as focused as they were on nabbing and training graduate students.

I had been second reader of several dissertations at Harvard, but Keith was the first graduate student who would be identified in the profession as my student. Over my years at UC, I worked with a few others like Keith, and working with them was a great joy, and a source of real pride—and a lot of fun. But with all of them, I worried. I worried that they would get chewed up in the same way I had gotten chewed up. I worried that I was responsible for sending them out into a profession that had gone a bit insane, where the ever-increasing pressure to publish would take over their lives. They were, of course, adults, responsible for their own decisions, and we often talked candidly about the pitfalls they would face.

But as much as I enjoyed the graduate students with whom I worked closely, I could not agree with the priorities of an institution that put their needs, however promising they might be, ahead of the needs of thousands upon thousands of undergraduates. Graduate students are, in a way, replicas of oneself, something that can be produced, certified, and *counted*—so the production of graduate students is of a piece with the rest of the system. They are part of a mania for quantitative measures of success—one can produce graduate students in the same way as one produces publications. And of course, grad students are cheap labor—as teaching fellows, graders, research assistants.

Thus, American academia has been corporatized. There is a bottom line (number of entries on those biobibs, number of new PhDs), and economic rationality has triumphed in perhaps the one institution where it should be subordinate to other values. We have subjected ourselves to the logic of the market—if something can't be tallied up and ranked, it doesn't exist. Academia has succumbed to the fiction that only *products* are real, as the late, great, Tony Judt put it. A well-taught class, stimulating new lectures instead of old notes, a new seminar, time spent mentoring students, a faculty reading group, organizing a conference, reviewing a manuscript for a publisher—these things can't be objectively measured. They are not products, and so they do not count.

If only products are real, then only the people who create them are important, and only certain institutions, filled with such people, deserve respect and status. It's not a huge leap from the logic of capital markets and CEO salaries to the salaries paid college and university presidents and academic stars, not a huge leap from the stagnant salaries of most everyone else caught up in global capitalism to the ways in which states and the federal government starve institutions of higher education when budgets get tight, and sometimes even when they don't. Faculty members like to think they stand outside the world of market forces, but nothing could be further from the truth.

There is one more point to make here, though it was not a factor for me. Most faculty members begin their climb up the academic ladder in their late twenties or around age thirty, and then are given somewhere between five and eight years to publish enough to earn tenure. It should be obvious that these are prime childbearing years for those who intend to have children. Thus the academic system puts maximum pressure on women, especially, but men as well, and on their partnerships and marriages, at the point in life when many will want to start a family. Judith Shklar confided to me at one point that she was glad she was kept on at Harvard as a part-time lecturer for many years before being given a full-time appointment. It allowed her, she said, both to do her work and to have children. "I couldn't have done it otherwise," she said one day over lunch. I had already moved to California and was back in Cambridge briefly. We had wine with lunch to celebrate her election as the first female president of the APSA. "There's a reason there hasn't been a woman president yet," she said matter-of-factly. I wondered how many women in academia, how many deans and university presidents, would have been surprised by her comments.

None of this is to argue that research and publication, or peer review, are unimportant. Should one need to do original, publishable research in some format, validated by one's peers, to earn tenure, or promotion to full professor after tenure? Absolutely, yes. Should there be some form of post-tenure review? Yes. But do we really need perpetual evaluation and so many articles and books, most of which do nothing but gather dust? Is there really only one way to be a scholar?

Slowly, haltingly, at first with a sense of dread, all of this became clear to me over time. Together with my social isolation from my department colleagues and a less-than-ideal teaching environment, I realized I had to look elsewhere for sustenance.

There was the theatre. I began reading books on Zen—this was California, after all. Acceptance. Suffering. Detachment. Separating oneself from one's thoughts and emotions. Seemed like it might be helpful. But then I took a class on meditation and was (mindfully) expelled—I would fall asleep while I was supposed to be concentrating on my breath.

But, even without meditation, I asked myself the question the institution presumed had only one answer: What is worth my time? Since I did not genuflect before the received deity, I had to find my own religion.

It turned out to be an eclectic faith, a hodge-podge . . . a little bit of this, a little bit of that. I published enough to get promoted to full professor and to keep my head above water. I did not divorce myself completely from orthodoxy, and I was not excommunicated. But the fun, the excitement, my energy were not with the received faith. I still tried to be a good soldier in my department, whatever my rank. I dutifully attended every department meeting, paid close attention, read the files of every job candidate. I learned a great deal from my razor-sharp colleagues. And semester by semester I learned to connect better with my students, despite class size and the financial pressures under which most of the undergraduates labored, leaving them little time and energy for their classes.

These students may not have had as much time to study as students in the Ivy League, and may not have been as well prepared for college-level work, but, as I adopted my teaching style to their level of preparation, I was gratified that I found myself able to reach them. In most classes there was a moment, about two or three weeks into the ten-week quarter, when things seemed to click—the students caught on, loosened up, started listening more carefully to what each other had to say, understood that there was no right or wrong answer to most of the most important questions about the cases we read. I worked hard for that click.

And gradually, some of them started showing up to office hours. *Do you think I could get into law school how do I prepare how much will it cost what courses should I take next year what about the LSAT what if I'm not sure what kind of law I want to practice do lawyers really work eighty hours a week how much can I make?* These were the years of the television series *LA Law*, and for the first time applications to law schools were exceeding applications to medical school.

I answered their questions and told them things I wished someone had told me when I was their age. *Maybe take a year or two off work in a related job figure out what you really want don't rush into anything unless you're sure and think about what kind of life you want not just your career. You have to love it, really love it, or it won't work.*

Love it really love it. I did love talking to those kids, and I loved reaching them in class. I loved the click. Lived for it, really.

All of this was positive, and I recognized that, given the awful state of the academic job market, I was in many ways lucky to be where I was. So I did benefit, a great deal, from being a member of this particular congregation, but I knew I would never be one of the church's elders, and all the bishops and deacons knew it as well.

Like the character she played in *Holiday*, Miss Kate began to suspect she would have to renounce respectability and find some other home.

By the fall of 1989, the beginning of my fourth year in California, I had a by-now predictable crisis and came close to giving up academia altogether. I had a one-quarter sabbatical, so decided to spend it in New York, looking for . . . I did not know what. Something else, something better. Like my brief flirtation with the idea of leaving Princeton and my brief romance in Boston with the idea of getting a second PhD, I had the impulse to flee, to start over, to find a better fit. Surely, I thought, there must be something better than having people count the number of pages I publish every two years, while teaching classes that are too large to students forced to work their way through college to pay ever-rising tuition, leaving them precious little time to do their work.

The APSA holds its annual meeting over the Labor Day weekend. By the time of the convention that year, I had arranged to sublet my apartment in San Diego and bought a plane ticket for New York. I had no place to stay there, but assumed I would deal with that in one way or another when I arrived. The plan was to fly to Atlanta for the APSA, return to San Diego to pack up, then take off for New York, where I would spend the sabbatical.

By 1989, some of us in the APSA had managed to organize an LGBT caucus. The profession was, on the whole, so conservative that our earliest meeting had been held in a private home away from the convention venues. That conference was in Washington, D.C., and I had dinner with two friends at a shady café far from the conference hotel before that first meeting. The whole thing felt a bit clandestine, as if we were about to commit espionage. Barney Frank showed up to the D.C. meeting, to everyone's surprise.

The nervousness continued beyond that first gathering. A meeting in a subsequent year was held in a basement at 10:00 p.m. Thousands had died, were still dying of AIDS, gay teenagers continued to commit suicide at three times the usual rate, but gay political scientists were so nervous we met in a basement. Only in 1989, much later than was the case in many other disciplines, were we ready to hold our first public, academic panels.

We held two that year. One was a roundtable discussion on *Bowers v. Hardwick*, the 1986 Supreme Court decision that had just validated state anti-sodomy laws, allowing states to blatantly criminalize same-sex behavior. The case was based on an incident that had occurred in Atlanta when a gay man was arrested for the crime of consensual sodomy with another adult in his own apartment. The police had legally entered the apartment, which made the case a perfect test case—or so everyone thought. Everyone was wrong.

I volunteered to chair the roundtable, and that was a big step, since the conference program would list the panel under the heading "LGBT Caucus" with my name prominently displayed as the chair. I was nervous, but my experiences at UCSD, my reaction to its bureaucratic strictures, had put me into a rebellious frame of mind, so I was ready for what became my full professional coming out. As I walked the halls of the conference hotel, there were a few sneers. One graduate student whom I had helped a bit at Harvard uttered a slur as I walked by. I felt a combination of amusement and dread—it reminded me of the reaction to my high school yearbook.

I assumed that, like many APSA panels, there would be perhaps ten people in the audience, or twenty if we were lucky. There were over fifty, and the panel was lively. I had invited Tom Stoddard, a well-known gay activist, to be on the panel, and his remarks were trenchant and moving; he spoke of how the fight for gay rights was deeply embedded in American values. I had also invited one of the *Hardwick* attorneys to attend, and she gave a riveting talk about the background of the case. I had invited Congressman Frank to appear, and he agreed. His name was printed in the program, which caught the attention of many, but at the last moment he canceled. Other speakers were equally good, and the Q and A was energized. I could feel in the room, see on people's faces, that this was a milestone of sorts.

I was thrilled. The panel had been successful. I had helped launch a gay presence within the APSA, however late.

I flew back to San Diego, made final arrangements with the person who was going to sublet my apartment, and said goodbye to friends on Labor Day.

But when the alarm went off that Tuesday morning, I could not make myself call a cab for the airport, and I think more than anything it was because of that APSA panel. It was worth doing, important in its own small way, and what did I think I would find in New York that would be equivalent? I had no work experience outside academia. My journalistic experience was, by then, quite dated. What did I think I would find, wandering the streets of New York?

As usual, I headed for the beach. I paced up and down and up and down, sometimes talking to myself, so much so some of the folks sitting at the water's edge looked at me funny. Why was I going to New York? Where did I expect to find a job—Wall Street?? What was I qualified to do outside of academia?? Did I think the *New York Times* would give me a column? No, this plan, if one could call it that, made no sense. No sense at all.

I missed the plane, unpacked, and told the renter that I would help him find another place to live. I decided that morning that I would finish my book and teach a course on gay politics, both as quickly as possible. I began looking for a condominium, and bought one within a few weeks.

Nose reapplied to the grindstone, I did finish the book, finally, and it seemed to have the right number of pages. In the last stages of writing it, I felt, finally, like I had something original to say. I got promoted to full professor. And then I spent a good bit of time and energy planning the course on gay politics.

The first time I taught it, it created quite a stir. The course was packed and I had to turn away a large number of students. I wrote careful lectures that I practiced delivering on a tape recorder.

I organized the course around the theme of mainstream versus radical politics. In every generation since World War II, there has been a split in the LGBT community. One side argues that "we" are just like everyone else, but for this one tiny difference, and that we therefore deserve equal legal rights (the right to marry or serve in the military, for example), and that, when we achieve those rights, our work will be done. This is the mainstream, assimilationist position. On the other side are those who put forward a more radical critique of existing institutions and practices—for example, arguing that multiple amorous relationships are not only permissible but are a positive good, that society needs to recognize the validity of these kinds of social and familial arrangements, or arguing not just that the government needed to do something about the AIDS crisis but that healthcare is a right for all. Of course I'm oversimplifying, but the recurrence of this kind of split in the political arguments of the community, decade by decade, is striking.

Thinking, reading, teaching about this split, seeing it played out in real time in the AIDS crisis and in the debates about marriage and the military, made me think about my own politics in a way I never had before, and, to some extent at least, made me less willing to go along, accept things as they were. Would I *really* want to get married, if I had the chance? Was it *really* worth fighting for the right to serve in the American military—a hot issue as I started to teach the course? Isn't the militarism of the American empire something to oppose, not sustain? Why aren't we fighting for employment protection, to end bullying in schools and families, and for universal healthcare? And (while I'm at it) why is scientific research the only viable model at this giant university, one that is supposed to serve the people of the state?

As I was teaching the course, I got to know queer faculty in other departments, one of whom was the indomitable Judith Halberstam, who was quickly becoming a national figure in queer studies. With Judith and several other faculty members as well as graduate students— none in political science—I participated in a reading group on LGBT issues that, for several years running, provided the intellectual community I had not found in my own department. Judith and the others became my true colleagues.

As I said when I introduced her to a packed auditorium at Oberlin College not too long ago, there is no one from whom I have ever learned more than Judith. Although we didn't always agree—at times we fought like crazy—she was, and still is, a brilliant provocateur, in the best sense of the word. She can take the most innocent text or movie or political argument and "queer" it—zero in on its internal contradictions and its implications in a way I find absolutely dazzling.

After the reading group had been meeting for a while, we held a big conference; with Judith, I took the lead in organizing it. As anyone who has ever organized a conference knows, it's a lot of work. We secured funding, invited scholars and writers from all over, and took care of the dozens of necessary details. It was quite successful, with packed audiences and a huge buzz on and off campus. We called it "Gay/Lesbian/Queer: Knowledges and Identities for the 90s."

The keynote speaker was Eve Sedgwick, the reigning eminence in queer theory. I stood at the back of the auditorium and listened to her very moving lecture, which was built around a queer student of color who had died and also made reference to her own battle with breast cancer, a battle she would eventually lose. The filled-to-capacity auditorium was riveted. I stood at the back, drinking it all in.

None of the work on the conference, of course, counted at the time of my next merit review. Similarly, the Chancellor asked me to chair a committee on LGBT campus welfare, the outcome of which was the establishment of a campus resource center. That took even more time and energy, since various campus constituencies—students, staff, radical faculty, more moderate faculty—had conflicting ideas about what the center should be; there was a lot of fighting, and I had to play peacemaker. Again, this counted for nothing at merit time (although the Chancellor did shake my hand vigorously at the center's opening ceremonies).

"I'm becoming a professional faggot," I said to one gay friend, and that was true of my work both on and off the UCSD campus. The APSA asked me to chair its own status committee (Committee on the Status of Lesbians and Gays)—again, not something that got counted at UC— and during my term as chair that Committee fought for the inclusion on the editorial board of the *Review*—the profession's flagship journal— of a scholar with expertise in gay and lesbian politics.

It was a prolonged battle within the association. The editor of the *Review* at the time was adamantly opposed to the idea, for reasons I understood. She felt appointment to the editorial board should be based on academic merit, not identity or status. We argued that the two were not mutually exclusive. After a long, drawn out fight, with support from Elinor Ostrom, then president of the APSA—later to win a Nobel Prize—our argument was accepted and an appointment to the editorial board was made. (Ostrom won the Nobel Prize in economics, which says a great deal about the discipline of political science.)

The meeting of the APSA Council at which Ostrom announced her support of our proposal was a moment of high drama.

APSA Council meetings are very formal affairs. The Council is large, all APSA staff is present, and the large meeting table requires microphones, so the meetings resemble Congressional hearings. I was quite nervous, but became very still, as I usually do at important moments, and said my piece. It was touch and go until Ostrom indicated support, which was a thrilling moment. Ostrom, who taught at Indiana University, looked for all the world like an Indiana housewife—modest clothes, modest voice. No one expected her to be out front on this issue.

At the time it felt like all of these random things just kept happening, pulling me in the direction of LGBT activism. No doubt, I agreed to do all this work not only out of genuine interest, to fill a vacuum in my campus life, but also because at that moment I did not have much of a research agenda.

For an academic, certainly an academic at a major research university, to admit the lack of a research agenda at any point in a career is akin to a confession of first degree murder, but there is was, staring me in the face—an extraordinarily inconvenient truth.

I had said what I had to say about the process of constitutional interpretation in my second book. It had taken a long time, and I felt I had done a reasonable job of being original. That book was one of many in a crowded, well-worn field. Did the world really need another?

I had dutifully announced that my next project would be a book about the First Amendment. But after writing the first few papers and delivering them as conference papers and then getting them published, I hit a wall. These papers could have constituted a draft of the first half of a monograph, and the true believer would have pushed on and produced it. But what was the point? To add several years of labor into producing a book just for another line on my biobib and a modest salary increase? There were at least five other current books on the First Amendment, and many more from previous decades sitting, unread, on library shelves.

The crisis came late one Sunday night at the beginning of spring break, when I had promised myself I would start working on the next paper. I wrote the first few paragraphs and couldn't go on. I reread the paragraphs over and over. I had an outline, I knew what needed to come next. But I couldn't write the next sentence.

Instead, I paced the floors until 3:00 a.m.

Part of me thought: I was tenured, I was a full professor. If I didn't take control now of what I did and didn't spend time and energy doing, it would never happen.

And part of me thought: Just do your work.

On cue, in my few hours of fitful sleep, I dreamt of two recent movies: *The Fugitive*, where Harrison Ford is running, running, running, and *Sommersby*, where Richard Gere takes the place of a dead soldier after the Civil War, pretending to be someone he isn't. I didn't have the Technicolor accouterments, but I was trying to make an important decision about my own small world. I didn't want to pretend, and I wanted to run away from something.

For the rest of spring break, I was agitated, unsure, angry at myself. Why was this so hard for me? Why couldn't I just proceed with a project I had started? Was I just lazy? Was I entering middle-age torpor? Had I been lulled into a Southern California stupor of pleasantness? For whatever else it is (exciting, exhilarating, interesting), the day-to-day experience of "doing" scholarship is seldom pleasant. Was this what a midlife crisis felt like? Had I been a good boy too long, ever since first grade, so now, finally, I was rebelling, a long-delayed adolescence?

Maybe so. Maybe I *was* finally rebelling, or getting a bit lazy in the California sun, now that I was safe, for who can possibly be safer than a tenured full professor? Maybe like Kate in *Summertime*, I needed to relax, to stop working so hard, at least for a little while. To risk falling into a canal in Venice.

Of course, that scene with the canal gave the real Hepburn a permanent ear infection, which plagued her for the rest of her life, but I didn't want to think about that.

Whatever the explanation, whatever was taking hold of me, it had been incubating for quite a long time, and I seemed to have finally lost the ability to beat it back.

Gritted teeth isn't working,

I wrote in my journal, as I put my notes on the First Amendment away. I gave up, at least for a while, the idea of another book on Supreme Court doctrine and instead started thinking about ways I could develop a research project on gay politics. It was a new field and it felt like there were unanswered questions there, work worth pursuing.

And I can see, now, that living through the plague, watching friends and acquaintances die in these early years, contributed to my decision. Gay lives, gay politics mattered, and academia needed to pay attention. Soon I began a collaborative project with a colleague, a former graduate student at the Santa Barbara campus on whose dissertation committee I sat, on political attitudes in the LGBT community.

Being gay, all my gay activism, the queer theory I had been reading in the faculty reading group—all contributed to what was coming in perhaps another way, not only to the choice of subject.

There are those who argue that being gay can force you to ask hard questions in all areas of your life. The culture's default assumption is heterosexuality, so one needs to ask: Is that really me? And then certain kinds of questions become just like peanuts or potato chips—hard to stop after just one. So you start to ask, about everything: Why do we do it (whatever "it" is) this way and not that way? And, often the most dangerous question, who says? Who wrote this script? As historian Martin Duberman, a gay pioneer, puts it, when you grow up and live outside the rules, without the comfort of living within social norms, when you push against boundaries, not just sexuality but everything else is open to question. To be gay, Duberman says, is to be a "potential saboteur." In a very different context, Hannah Arendt speaks, in one of her earliest works, of the necessity for someone who finds herself part of a minority group to consider the cost of fitting in, to become a "conscious pariah."

Of course I faced nothing remotely as momentous and life-threatening as Arendt's crisis as a Jew in Germany before World War II—although we should not forget that, before the modern gay rights movement, members of sexual minority groups were in fact sometimes murdered, often imprisoned, subjected to electroshock, or confined to mental hospitals. We should not forget that there are parts of the world, and even parts of America, where murder because of sexual orientation happens still.

I was lucky; I never faced harsher forms of discrimination. And I am younger than Duberman by twenty years. What he experienced in the 1950s, I experienced in the 1970s, when American life was finally beginning to open up for sexual minorities. But I certainly experienced milder forms of homophobia, and even a whiff of anti-Semitism here and there, and I seemed to have the same gene that Duberman and Arendt are talking about, the one that leads to pacing the floor until 3:00 a.m.

That gene has turned out to be something of a mixed blessing. Instead of silence, one speaks . . . and speaks and speaks and speaks. The combination of that gene and the security of tenure made me perhaps too quick to fight with colleagues, unwilling to choose my battles or let others have their way. To be sure, that gene, plus tenure, helped me choose a new project and teach new courses, which I needed to do to revive my sense of excitement about my profession, and that was all to the good. But it has also had a downside. At UCSD this didn't really matter; everyone spoke their mind and fought for what they wanted. . . . I fit right in. But later, in a different context, my style would help get me into hot water.

But for now, I charged ahead with the new gay project. My collaborator and I faced a serious methodological challenge, in that it's impossible to randomly sample that community in survey research. We did our best to finesse that problem by using mailing lists of organizations and other proxies in four cities. We were able to write several articles, with interesting but tentative conclusions, based on the data we did manage to collect (for example, that members of the LGBT community who labeled themselves "queer" were more supportive of fighting for marriage equality, not less, as commonly believed). But this was not a project that was going to result in a Big, Important Book, or dozens of articles.

So to a certain degree as a holding action, I agreed to chair the political science department. Department chairs work hard—all those memos, reviewing one's colleagues—and aren't expected to get as much research done as otherwise—a reprieve of sorts. And I thought I might enjoy the job. I had enjoyed the administrative work I had done up to that point—Head Tutor at Harvard, director of the undergraduate program and pre-law advisor at UCSD—so I thought, why not chair?

I did enjoy it, in a way. The work of a scholar and a teacher is often quite solitary. One spends long hours reading, writing, preparing, and, usually, only a few hours per week interacting with other human beings, in classes, in meetings. Being an administrator is much more social. One spends many more hours with one's colleagues, with the staff, with students, and in endless meetings. I also found that being an administrator required putting theoretical politics into action, and was, on that level, intellectually interesting. As a chair one spends a lot of time bargaining, negotiating, persuading, budgeting—all political processes I had studied. Being an administrator was for me, in part, translating theory into action.

Stepping back, devising a strategy for best getting a bunch of smart people, who are trained to find the flaw in every argument, from Point A to Point B, requires some thought and some creativity. For example, when I became chair, I discovered that up until that point, everyone had been allowed to spend whatever they needed to spend on office expenses—xeroxing, long distance phone calls, that sort of thing. Not surprisingly, that led to deficits as the department added new members. So I formed a budget committee, had it come up with a recommendation, put the department's most stellar young scholar on the committee, and had him present the committee's recommendations at a special meeting, where I was sure there was food. Everyone agreed to set spending limits.

As chair at UCSD, however, it was also my job to administer the system of personnel review, which only solidified my sense of the basic craziness of the system. In talks with colleagues about upcoming merit reviews, I saw that I was not the only one chafing under the system. And in dealing with issues of salary and research funds, I learned who had been given what, which only further convinced me that there really were two classes of citizens at UC, and that the system masked this through its supposedly open procedures and superficially egalitarian ethos. Everyone was on the same salary scale, except those who weren't. Everyone was eligible for the same basic research funds, except those who got more, in decisions made not by the Committee on Research but by one senior administrator alone. The differences were sometimes mind-boggling.

Everyone was equal at UCSD, except some were more equal than others.

Now it may be that much higher salaries and much higher research funding are appropriate for the most well-known members of the faculty, that the sky should be the limit. It's certainly possible to argue that point of view. But, I thought, if UC accepts that argument, it should do so openly, and admit that, like the richest private universities—indeed like the rest of society—it has become a star system, where the top tier gets rich while everyone else muddles along (at best). It should give up the pretense of its salary scale, the public numbers known to the Regents and the press.

As chair I also presided over a case in which my colleagues denied tenure to an Assistant Professor, unjustly in my view. His work was very good, new, interesting, published in respected venues, but ... what? Not sufficiently cutting edge. Perhaps we could do better.

Telling him the result of our deliberations was one of the hardest things I've ever had to do, especially since I thought that the case represented the worship of the Great God Research carried to absurd lengths. I will always remember how I felt driving home after that conversation. I hated what we had done and I hated myself for being a part of it. I hated the system even more. That night I couldn't sleep, watched movies long after midnight.

As I continued through my four-year term as chair, it became clear that going back to teaching and research full time when my term ended was not going to be a great option. I needed a change.

Luckily, I found an alternative.

When I gave UCSD a chance to retain me, not surprisingly, it chose not to. It was clear to everyone, including me, that I didn't really fit, that I would never be truly valued by the institution. Miss Kate, swallowing hard, took a good long look at herself, just as she had in *The Philadelphia Story* (alas, there was no Cary Grant to help her along). She decided to move on.

But. Like most of those who renounce a religion, there are always moments when I miss it, feel twinges of doubt, wonder whether it would have been better to stay in the congregation.

I needed to make the final decision about going back to UCSD (technically, I took a leave, and could have returned) during a week in which I attended a conference at the Hague, presenting some of the first, tentative research findings on gay politics that we had uncovered. All the way to the Netherlands and back, I fretted ... what should I do? On the flight home I paced up and down the aisle so much the stewards seemed to suspect I was a terrorist and sternly asked me to take my seat.

When I got home, there was an email waiting for me from the colleague who had replaced me as UCSD chair. The Committee on Research, which had been providing most of the funds necessary to conduct our gay project—as it funded everyone on campus with modest sums every year—had turned us down for a renewal of the grant. Why? Because we had not yet published any of the findings from our work.

"But we're still collecting data," I replied. "Do they expect us to publish results before we collect all the data?" Presenting tentative findings in an unpublished conference paper was one thing. Publishing those results would have been another, and seriously irresponsible.

The answer came back loud and clear: Yes. No more funds until you start publishing.

"Um, isn't that a Catch-22? If we can't finish collecting data, we can't publish."

I got nowhere, as usual, and that made the decision easier.

I told my colleague I would not be coming back.

8

DRAMA: ADVANCED SEMINAR

Y ou must be losing your marbles," a colleague said to me over lunch on yet another impossibly perfect Southern California day in the spring of 2000. "It may be time to call the men in the white coats."

Like Julia Roberts in *Mona Lisa Smile*, I had come to idealize small colleges. Not a giant mega-versity obsessed with research, but, at least in my fantasy, a small institution where teaching and nurturing bright, eager students was the essential goal, not a nuisance to be borne. Like Julia, I was about to leave sunny California for such a place, trading the sun for a state with lots of snow.

My UCSD colleague was incredulous. Everyone was. Moving from a major university to a small college was one of those things that just didn't happen very often in academia; usually people tried to move in the opposite direction. Universities were where the action was, where reputations were made, the big league. The top few small colleges— Swarthmore, Amherst, Williams—were ok, the general thinking went, but beyond that . . . no. Small potatoes. The minor league.

And then there was the matter of my age. I was rapidly approaching 50, and friends wondered if it was too late to adjust to such a big change. "You're too fragile for a move this big," one of my close friends, a precise mathematician, said to me over Thai food, trying to persuade me to turn down the job. Having survived fourteen years at UC, the last four of them as chair of a large, cantankerous department, I didn't think of myself as particularly fragile, so I was mostly amused at my friend's armchair psychologizing. "I'll manage," I said, smiling.

149

I should have paid more attention. I wasn't fragile, but I had spent decades in the major league, as it were, and was used to its customs, its rules, its practices. Baseball is baseball, I thought—how different could it really be?

I found out. It could be really, really different.

The new position was at Macalester College in St. Paul, Minnesota. I was interested in the job in part because there are very few small colleges located in large cities. Most American colleges were founded at a time when inculcating morality and Christian virtue was a central goal, and thus avoiding the sin and degradation of cities was seen as essential to the college mission. As a result, many American liberal arts colleges are in the middle of nowhere, far from what was considered corrupting civilization. So when a college in a city expressed an interest in me for an endowed chair, I didn't feel I could ignore it.

They flew me out for an interview in mid-April, and I was stunned by how cold it was. After fourteen years in California, I had grown unused to winter (and mid-April is often still winter in Minnesota). I spent a weekend exploring the city before the interview on Monday and Tuesday, and despite having grown up there, the Midwest had become a stranger to me. Everything looked weird and exotic: the houses, the building materials, the people.

For the interview on campus I had been asked to deliver a talk about my research, which went well, and they also asked me to teach a class. I contacted the person teaching the class, an adjunct, to coordinate the reading for the day, and we spoke several times. Yet when I got to the classroom I discovered that the students hadn't read the cases they needed to have read for my lecture to make any sense. "Well actually," the adjunct said cheerily, they've read X, Y, and Z, not A, B, and C.

Total panic. I didn't understand how the adjunct could have gotten things so wrong after several email messages and conversations, and I half suspected, or feared, that this was deliberate sabotage. Perhaps, she thought, if she could make sure I messed up in the classroom, she would get rehired for another year.

After dark thoughts like that raced through my head at 150 miles per hour, I considered telling the chair it would be impossible to teach the class (most faculty in the department were sitting in). But instead I plunged forward, talking off the top of my head, asking the students questions, and somehow it worked, or worked well enough.

They offered me the job, and I had a big decision to make.

I wasn't sold on the place. UCSD, for all its faults, was a well-known and respected research university. Macalester, on the other hand, was not in the top tier of American liberal arts colleges. Many people had never heard of it, or didn't know where it was. Some confused it with McMaster, a university in Ontario. "How will you teach American politics in Canada?" one colleague asked.

I thought about what I would be giving up and what I would be gaining in return. Up to that point in my academic life I had stayed on script. Michigan, Princeton, Harvard, the University of California—all of a piece, all known for serious scholarship, all prestigious—all part of the academic establishment. But a small liberal arts college in Minnesota that many had never heard of? I was going to leave the Yankees for the Carolina league and the Durham Bulls?

Adding to my uncertainty was a bizarre negotiation with the Macalester Provost, who initially offered me a salary lower than my UC salary, and argued strenuously, and at great length, that I should accept it. "That's the strangest thing I've ever heard," a senior colleague from whom I sought advice said about the weird phone call and salary offer. I held firm, and for a few days it looked as if the whole thing had collapsed, but, after I sent a series of blistering letters to members of the search committee, the Provost finally raised his offer, matching what I was already earning. At UCSD I had gotten good at blistering.

Prestige places haven't exactly been cozy homes for me,

I conceded in my journal, and that was the argument that cinched it, despite the bizarre negotiations. Perhaps I wasn't Hepburn in *Woman of the Year*, one of a kind, brilliant, accomplished. Perhaps I was Kate in *Summertime*, a more average schoolteacher, still smart and cultured (and very well dressed), but someone who really did belong in the Midwest. Perhaps Macalester College in St. Paul, Minnesota would be right for me.

Then too, the University of Minnesota was right near Macalester, and I knew people there. I was fairly confident I would be able to arrange an adjunct appointment. And so it seemed like I might be heading for a perfect balance: A chair at a liberal arts college and perhaps the opportunity to occasionally teach graduate students at a fine university.

I had always heard good things about the Twin Cities, however different they may have been from Southern California, and enjoyed them when I had visited once or twice. Minnesota was known for progressive politics and lots of culture. Altogether it felt like a package that would be hard to reproduce elsewhere. And I was getting older—how many other offers might be coming?

I arrived by way of Chicago, where I spent a few days with my sister and her family. It was early September and, as usual in Chicago, hot and muggy, so I was sweating and wearing shorts when I got on the plane for the short flight to Minnesota. When I got off the plane and drove the short distance into St. Paul, it was thirty degrees cooler. Even by Minnesota standards, they were having an unusually frosty fall.

St. Paul, where my paternal grandmother had once lived, was a city of small, well-established neighborhoods, old houses, and Summit Avenue, the longest stretch of Victorian architecture in the country, at the end of which stood the St. Paul cathedral, a smaller version of the Vatican, on top of a grand hill. Driving down the Avenue and coming upon the cathedral produced a strange sensation, almost an out-of-body experience—one was suddenly transported from the quintessential middle American city to feudal Europe.

As modern Europe struggled with mad cow disease and the Vermont legislature legalized same-sex civil unions, I unpacked and tried to get acclimated.

The Macalester campus stretched over several blocks on both sides of Grand Avenue, one of St Paul's other major thoroughfares, though not usually terribly busy. There was a handsome central quadrangle around which sat most of the main buildings, including an oddly shaped, modern glass chapel built by the Weyerhaeuser family in 1969, the site of most large meetings and assemblies. It looked a bit like Philip Johnson's famous Connecticut glass house, but on steroids, with an incongruous cross perched on top of one of its many sides. On another corner of the main quad, a brand-new, lovely, very expensive student center opened while I was there, and in an opposite corner sat Carnegie, where my department and classrooms were housed. The floors on the stairs were rubber to absorb the wear and tear of hundreds of boots during the slush season, which was long, very long.

The physical space of the department had a nice feel. Faculty offices were arrayed around a large central area where the one department staff person worked, and there were couches and computer stations where students would sometimes gather between or after classes. Faculty members taking a break from work, or just passing through, could josh with Roxy, the all-knowing department secretary, or with students. One of my favorite students, a young woman in a wheelchair, was sometimes there. One day I heard her talking to another student, who asked her how she was doing.

"I feel like killing myself," she said. The end of the semester, with paper deadlines and finals, was approaching.

"Don't do it here," I called through my open office door, and everyone laughed.

The students at Macalester were wonderful, and I loved teaching them. Classes were small, lively, and a joy to teach. The students actually did the reading, came prepared to talk about it, happily engaged in the give and take that makes constitutional law such a lively subject. They apologized when they missed a class, which astounded me. I was immediately impressed with them and plunged in with both feet. *I get so much from the kids,* I happily recorded in my journal.

I loved playing devil's advocate as we discussed the legal cases we read, and, as usual, no matter which way a student responded, I pushed in the opposite direction. Sometimes though I couldn't help myself and revealed what I really thought, and I found that happening more often at Macalester. Among my favorite cases are the ones dealing with Christmas decorations, and whether their display on public property violates the Establishment Clause of the First Amendment. There are always students who argue that these situations present no constitutional difficulty. Some of the cases involve not just candy canes and snowflakes but blatantly religious symbols, such as a crèche—a depiction of the birth of Christ—displayed in a town square or in a government building.

"Well, it's not really religious," some poor student will always argue. "I mean, it's just something that shows that it's the holiday season, like a Christmas tree."

"So you're telling us," I say, all but rolling up my sleeves, "that BABY JESUS in his manger is not a religious symbol?"

The student who spoke starts slowly sliding under his seat.

"And it's called a *Christmas* tree, but it's not a religious symbol. How, exactly, do you figure that?"

Bright red face, an open mouth, and a futile attempt to speak.

"You wouldn't by any chance be a member of America's large, powerful Christian majority, would you?"

Then some other student takes over, argues the position, goes in for the final kill. The exchange illustrates the most important thing about constitutional rights—that they are there for the minority, that majority rule should not always carry the day, and that majorities do not always realize what they are doing.

They get it, and the poor student hiding under his seat recovers. It was the kind of interchange that made the classroom come alive, and Macalester seemed like a perfect place to do what I do. During my first few weeks of teaching, it felt like I had been transported back to my earliest experiences as a graduate student at Princeton. I felt the same sense of excitement as I watched my students' faces, listened to them, pushed them this way or that, got them arguing with each other. At the beginning, at least, it felt like I had finally found a congenial home. My personality, my teaching style, the material I chose, all came together in a way it hadn't in a long time.

As a bonus, I was able to teach a broader range of subjects than I had been teaching at UCSD or Harvard, including American political thought, which I had wanted to teach for a long time. UCSD and Harvard are large enough that I had colleagues who taught American political thought, while I was expected to concentrate on con law—an example of the hyper-specialization of the modern research university. At smaller colleges, one could range more broadly. I was also able to teach a course on gender, sexuality, and the law, which would have been too specialized a topic at UCSD, and a seminar on democratic theory, which, again, at a larger place would have been in a colleague's portfolio rather than in mine.

I reveled in being able to branch out to teach new subjects. Preparing them—and having the College regard that as work worth doing, rather than a distraction—was one of the great benefits for me of moving to a smaller place. The College even gave me a semester off to prepare, and that recharged my intellectual batteries in a major way. I loved the new material, and was grateful for the opportunity to prepare it.

And, just like Julia, I enjoyed getting to know my students. Some needed help choosing a major, some needed help thinking through career choices. Some just wanted to talk. Office hours were always crowded. The vast majority of students who come to a small liberal arts college really are there to learn. They take their classes seriously, they do the work, they are willing and anxious to engage, and they are responsive. In the Macalester classroom and in its students, it seemed as if I had finally found my calling at a place that wanted and valued what I had to offer.

That has been the upside of small colleges for me. Alas, as Miss Julia discovered in *Sleeping with the Enemy*, danger can lurk just underneath a placid, well-appointed surface, and people who seduce you can take off the gloves and start throwing punches in five seconds flat.

The chilliness I felt on landing in the Twin Cities never really dissolved, at least with my colleagues, despite my best efforts. At the two liberal arts colleges where I have worked, in fact, I have discovered that small colleges can be intense theatres of conflict and jealousy. The personalization of disagreement, sometimes to the point of vindictiveness, together with plain, old fashioned dishonesty, are, if not exactly rampant, then certainly prominent.

Who knew.

Some signs of trouble at Macalester surfaced the moment I arrived. I was asked to deliver an inaugural lecture for my endowed chair; I was the chair's first occupant, and this was, for a small campus, a big event, followed by a luncheon. In the audience were trustees, faculty, alumni, students. Of course, my department colleagues attended, and when they walked in and I saw the look on some of their faces, cold sweat started trickling down my torso. I could tell by their expressions and body language they were not happy to be there, not happy at all.

The chair I occupied was named in honor of Ted Mitau, a refugee from Hitler who eventually became a much-loved faculty member at Macalester, so I used the occasion to talk about the ways in which being an outsider can shape one's political perspective. I talked about Mitau's life, and also the lives of two other European refugees who had played an important role in my life in one way or another, Felix Frankfurter and Judith Shklar. I also talked about my own biography and came out, talking about what it had meant for me to be a gay academic. LGBT faculty and students were thrilled, but former Second Lady of the United States Joan Mondale, a trustee, looked as if she were choking on a lemon.

Oh my, I thought as I tried to stick to my text, glancing past her to my frowning, uncomfortable-looking colleagues . . . the natives are not nearly as friendly as I thought.

Soon after the lecture, I discovered my department was being torn apart by a conflict centering around its most junior member, whom I liked very much and was told I would be expected to mentor. She had just had a large chunk of her appointment transferred to another program; she would now have a joint appointment, and the other program would have a majority of her time. There was a serious conflict between her and two senior political scientists, and her appointment had been shifted to protect her.

It was a huge mess. Charges were hurled back and forth, and everyone was upset and tense.

The conflict, and the loss of a share of her time, was a crisis for the department and also for the College, since the young woman would soon face her tenure decision. In such a small place there was no way for me to avoid hearing everyone's account of what was going on. I tried to listen and be sympathetic to all involved, which probably satisfied no one. By the time it was all over my dominant impression was that the conflict should never have reached the point that it did, and that the fact that it had gotten so out of hand indicated that something, somewhere was greatly amiss. She had not been treated well—that much seemed clear to me.

Worse, from my point of view, was that I learned that the conflict had broken out while the job offer to me was pending, but no one had bothered to tell me what was going on. Before accepting the position the previous spring, I had flown back to Minnesota to spend more time getting a feel for the place. I met with faculty, with the Provost, with the College President. They could have, should have, informed me of what was happening, or at least hinted at it, which would have allowed me to ask the right questions, but no one said a word about the huge drama being played out right at that moment. All smiles, I was told the young woman's appointment was being shifted because it would provide a "better fit" for her. Underneath the smiles, I soon discovered, was this roiling disaster.

If I had been given an inkling of what was happening, I would have turned down the job—which, I'm sure, they realized. I was joining a department of only six other permanent members (only now it was five and two-fifths). Being in a department that small is a bit like participating in a group marriage, and this particular marriage was clearly troubled from the moment I walked in the door—indeed, from the moment our courtship became serious.

And there were other rumblings. On the surface my department colleagues were usually friendly, but I noticed a tone of condescension, sometimes, when we spoke about this or that, a defensiveness, a smidgen of resentment buried just under the surface. After all the therapy I had had, after all the psychology I had studied, I knew how to read subtle clues—tone of voice, body language. I detected, from the very beginning, especially among the middle-level faculty, a whiff of jealousy, a what-makes-you-so-great attitude that reminded me of the reaction of some of my fellow graduate students at Princeton when I was offered the job at Harvard. At Macalester I had been brought in at a high level, and I sensed that the associate professors, especially, found that galling, to have someone plopped down in their midst who outranked them.

I tried to conjure how my colleagues looked at me. I could imagine that they probably thought of me as extraordinarily fortunate—and they were right, I had been. I was able to spend my first two decades at research universities, where the teaching load was light and I was able to establish my professional reputation, such as it was. Just to take the most obvious example of the kind of time-gobbling work done by small college faculty: Never once in all those years at universities was I required to grade undergraduate papers or exams in a large class—there were always graduate-student graders available to do that work. Then, after that relatively privileged existence, I was able to step back and make a conscious decision to shift gears.

Had I started my career at a small college, I would either have had to forgo a good bit of my research, or it would have taken much longer to complete, or I would have needed to work twice as hard as I did—as many do at small colleges. I have enormous respect for those who do both, and I could see that most of my colleagues at Macalester did both, and did both well.

Perhaps their realization that I had had it easy for so long contributed to their coolness toward me as a colleague. They might have resented the fact that someone who had had it easy in the major league could be rewarded with an endowed chair at a different kind of institution. I could see the logic of that. I probably would have felt the same way myself.

Whatever the source of the various tensions in the department, my response was to become as friendly as I knew how to be. I tried to turn myself into Holly Golightly, inviting everyone to the party. I invited people to have lunch, dinner, tea, drinks. On election night—Bush v. Gore, 2000—I took the department chair and his wife out to dinner, while the restaurant buzzed about the election and the waitresses gave bulletins every few minutes from the radio in the kitchen. Now that I owned a house, I gave parties—spending a fortune on catering, since I had never really mastered cooking and entertaining had never been my thing. My first party was a combined house-warming and holiday party in December. I invited about sixty people and was so nervous I ordered enough food and liquor for two hundred. I ate leftover cheesecake for weeks, and I still have one of the unopened bottles of brandy.

I feel a bit like Mrs. Dalloway,

I confided in my journal on that very cold December night, nervous and anxious and needing the party to be a success. I was worried that the weather would keep people away, not yet having learned that weather that would prompt most cities to shut down means nothing in Minnesota. People came, and seemed to have a good time, though once again there was some awkwardness with some of my department colleagues, two of whom stood in a corner and seemed uncomfortable.

I also held several dinner parties, especially at first. For one of them, the caterer never arrived, and I ran to the nearest grocery store and grabbed whatever I could find to throw together something that resembled a meal: melon and pasta and chocolate cake for dessert. I was a wreck, but no one seemed to notice anything was amiss, except Patsy, the sweet golden retriever I had just adopted, whom I forgot to feed until everyone had left. Altogether those first years I was more social than I had ever been, not just with my department colleagues but with colleagues I met throughout the college.

Very little came of my efforts, with the exception of one or two friendships I made with faculty outside political science. Hardly anyone reciprocated with an invitation. As time passed and I continued to invite people who seldom invited me back, I could not figure out what was going on—had I violated some secret code of conduct? Or were people just too busy, too settled to socialize? One time it took four months to set up a lunch date with a colleague in another department, despite the fact that we worked in adjacent buildings and lived a few blocks from each other.

Eventually I came to think of the cold shoulder as a repetition of the single-gay-man syndrome I had experienced at UCSD, magnified by the smallness of a small college. Everybody at a small college knows everyone, and everybody knows everybody's personal story down to the most specific details. At one campus event soon after I arrived, I overheard someone say about me, "You mean he doesn't have a partner?"

Or perhaps it was just the fact of being new, being an outsider. Most everyone else seemed to have been in Minnesota forever. One friend from outside the College, a transplanted New Yorker, told me it took her more than ten years before people became at all friendly, and this despite the fact that she married into a prominent political family. Garrison Keillor (whom I would occasionally see at the grocery store) knows whereof he speaks when he describes the strange insularity of Lake Wobegon, and he's not exaggerating very much at all.

I did my best to create a social life for myself both outside the College and within; outside with some success, inside, mostly failing.

But day to day at the College, I immersed myself in teaching, and was more than happy to do so. I lived by the rhythm of the classroom, teaching in the morning, preparing the next day's class in the afternoon, reading in the evening. It was a rhythm that suited me, and on cold nights in front of the fire (a good seven months of the year in Minnesota), it felt like I was where I belonged. My classes were lively and fun to teach. Although I continued to pursue scholarship, it wasn't the only thing that mattered, and the pace at which I produced it seemed to be sufficient—no one was counting the number of pages. I was beginning to feel settled.

Soon, though, the young woman's tenure case was upon the department. Given the conflict surrounding it and the fact that I arrived late on the scene and was therefore untainted, I was the only member of the political science department to serve on the tenure committee. My other colleagues had no way of knowing what position I took on the matter, but the young woman did in the end receive tenure. It was assumed I supported her.

I was never forgiven; most of my other colleagues wanted her gone. Her appointment was then moved entirely out of the department.

To compound the problem in my colleague's eyes, I was made chair of the department soon after arriving—much too soon, as it turned out. Fatefully, I made the mistake of changing some department practices.

For example, the outgoing chair seldom took votes. I asked for voting rules—I had never been in a department without them—and everyone agreed, perhaps not realizing the impact this would have. Especially when it came to hiring decisions, which now required a two-thirds majority, as it had at UCSD, this meant that, at times, some department members did not always get their way, since search committees were large and included some students as well as faculty from other departments.

Tensions seemed to develop over the simplest matter. On one occasion, I had scheduled a department meeting for noon (as usual). That morning, two colleagues told the department secretary they could not be there . . . so I canceled the meeting. Another colleague took the occasion, in an email to everyone, to say the cancellation raised questions about the department's new leadership, that there was a danger that I was "undoing" the "hard work" all of them had put into building the department.

One canceled meeting and disaster loomed.

Emails became increasingly hostile, especially when a search for a new department member resulted in deadlock. People were angry, truly angry (one colleague wrote that he was really "pissed off" and would "not forget" that I opposed his favored job candidate), and I couldn't understand why. Isn't this routine, I innocently wondered, a disagreement about job candidates?

I thought I knew how to be a colleague and a department chair. If enough people can't come to a meeting, fine, reschedule it. No big deal. If you disagree about a job candidate, say so. If a disagreement can't be bridged, so be it—take a vote and live with the results. If a search fails one year, repeat it the following year . . . happens all the time. Best to be cautious, and fairer to the candidate who would have to earn tenure, to have consensus—or at least two-thirds agreeing—before making what could be a thirty-year commitment to a new colleague. I didn't stop to think that procedures and practices that worked at a large research university might not work in a small pond like Macalester, or that I needed to be especially careful with the egos of my colleagues when things did not turn out as they wanted.

To be sure, there was some hubris in how I proceeded: I plunged right in. I asked for different procedures and put items on the agenda, all within a few months. I did not hesitate to disagree. I could have proceeded more cautiously, less swiftly, consulted people one by one, been more sensitive to the emotional temperature of my colleagues. My attitude was, *well, okay, you want me to chair, here's what I think needs to happen*. I was busy, very busy, teaching new courses, and didn't give a lot of thought to how to be chair. I thought my experience was enough.

Big Mistake.

To aggravate the damage I was unwittingly doing, in addition to being appointed chair I was appointed to the committee to find a new College President after the resignation of Mike McPherson. At a small college, such things are very real measures of status, and again, in small but noticeable ways, I could see the resentment building among my colleagues.

The presidential search was yet another source of drama. The committee consisted of six trustees, three members of the faculty, and representatives of alumni and the non-teaching staff. One experience during the search—or perhaps I should say my interpretation of one experience—had a profound effect on me.

One of the candidates for the presidency was named Rosenberg, and he had a clear New York accent. His record was impressive and he performed quite well in the early round of interviews, and most members of the committee were enthusiastic about his candidacy as he advanced from round to round. But two trustees were not happy.

"He seems awfully pushy," one said.

"Yes, he's very New York," the other added.

This reminded me of second grade. Now class, what's the next word in this sequence: Pushy New York . . .

Jew! That's correct!

These sorts of comments continued, especially from one trustee, and grew even more explicit, as Mr. Rosenberg survived each round of interviews and became a finalist. One of my faculty colleagues on the committee interpreted the remarks just as I did, and was just as shocked, so I knew I was not imagining things. The committee met in a Minneapolis hotel, often late into the evening, and, driving back to St. Paul, exhausted and upset, we tried to figure out what to do about what we were hearing.

One Saturday night the committee met late into the evening after interviewing the dwindling number of surviving candidates earlier in the day. We took a break around 10:30, and one of the trustees good-naturedly said, as we reassembled, "we can't stay all night, tomorrow is Macalester Sunday" at the local church (Macalester was founded as a Presbyterian institution, but, like many such colleges, it is now nondenominational).

"Well," one of the offending trustees said, so that everyone could hear, "it's really hard to imagine someone named ROSENBERG representing us at Macalester Sunday."

I had never experienced anything like this, at least not face-to-face. What was even worse than the remarks themselves was that no one in the room condemned the comments. I know that at least two other members of the committee, both trustees, interpreted the most blatant of the remarks as I did, since, sitting next to them, I heard their whispers back and forth about what was being said ("well he's Jewish," one of them said). That they did not cry foul was, I think, the most shocking part of what was happening.

There is a debate among those who study the First Amendment about whether hate speech should be protected. There are those who say it should not be, because it silences the victims, making it impossible for them to respond and to participate fully in whatever enterprise they are pursuing—school or work or community. On the other side are those who say hate speech is still speech and cannot be abridged. It may be morally abhorrent, but the remedy for bad speech is good speech, so this theory goes, and those affected have a right and duty to respond. Speech cannot be restricted because of its content, unless it turns into an immediate threat directed at a specific individual.

I had always defended the second position, and defended it strongly, both in my classes and outside. When the ACLU in San Diego was torn up over this issue, due to a recently passed speech code in the UC system, I fought (and lost) a fierce fight in favor of the second, more libertarian position.

Coming face-to-face with what seemed to me blatantly anti-Semitic speech at Macalester made me rethink. It's fair to say that it knocked the wind out of me; it came close to paralyzing me. I did not sleep for several nights. I remember vividly one morning when I had to force myself to get dressed and drive to the next meeting. I just simply did not want to walk into that room.

After the first few comments of this ilk, I prepared some remarks in case it happened again, but when it did, I literally could not open my mouth. I looked down at my notes but they might as well have been written in Sanskrit. And I had these reactions despite the fact that I was in an especially safe position. I was a tenured college professor. If I had told off the anti-Semite, nothing really horrible could happen to me.

But, pushy Jew though I may be, I could not speak.

What I did instead was go privately to the chair of the Board, who had been sitting in as a non-voting member at some of the meetings. He acknowledged that things had been said that should not have been said and assured me he would deal with it. "Gosh, this diversity stuff really is hard, isn't it," he said, in a perfect example of the style of speech known as Minnesota Nice. Gee whiz, I guess it is, I wanted to reply (but didn't). I decided to trust him—there was little alternative. The worst offender apparently defended himself by claiming that he was only worried that a Jewish president might be "uncomfortable." Could I prove otherwise? Of course not. But I knew what I heard, and so did my faculty colleague. I knew how it felt.

Back in my department, I continued to be as friendly as I could be (more parties, more dinners), but I was making little headway with my colleagues. I continued on the path of sin in their eyes, and the resentments soon erupted into civil war.

It turned out that my colleagues suddenly did not like what I was teaching. My courses were the same courses I described wanting to teach when I was interviewed for the position, and they received high evaluations from Macalester students, but apparently I was letting the department down. My other sins were raising a half million dollars to fund student-faculty research, in honor of our retiring colleague Chuck Green, and scheduling a number of department meetings to talk about the curriculum.

Chuck had taught the nuts and bolts of American politics to generations of Macalester students, often sending them out into the world, in one way or another, to collect data and to do research. To honor him, we decided, collectively, to raise money to fund such student research and student-faculty collaborations in the future. Perhaps not expecting me to raise very much, my colleagues who did not teach American politics were shocked when I brought in a donation of a half million dollars, and they suddenly characterized the effort as an attempt to feather my own nest. I had no designs on the money; it would have been useless in my courses.

This was strange enough, since our decision to raise money in honor of Chuck was collective. And then things became even stranger.

A year or two before I arrived, the department was evaluated by a committee of scholars from outside Macalester. Academic departments routinely undergo such program reviews every ten years or so. The committee looked at the department's elaborate set of four different introductory courses and commented that, although they were fine courses, the department did not have the personnel necessary to staff them. They said that it would be a challenge to staff them even with twice the number of faculty.

As chair, keeping an eye on rising enrollments—rising in part because the department was now larger—I quickly came to the same conclusion. My greatest sin, apparently, was calling this to the attention of my colleagues and suggesting we consider doing something about it.

This touched a nerve. *How dare you raise this issue you are destroying all of our hard work the problem isn't our curriculum the problem is you.*

Excuse me? Don't you want to look at these numbers?

No, they did not want to look at the numbers or talk about the visiting committee report. They wanted to yell at me.

The meeting quickly became tense. My colleagues attacked me and my courses, told me, in so many words, that I wasn't doing my job. Tempers flared, including mine. I cut the meeting short. It was not pleasant, but it was all pretty mild by research-university standards, and so I thought, *well, ok, fine, we all got things off our chests, now we can move on.*

I was wrong.

It turned out that two of my colleagues had already gone to the Provost to complain about me, and, after a bit more tawdry drama, the Provost removed me as chair.

P.F. Kluge is a writer and graduate of Kenyon College; he wrote a wonderful memoir about a year he later spent there as an instructor, *Alma Mater*. In it he says the currency of a small college is love.

That may be the case; if so, I wasn't getting any.

I didn't understand what all the fuss was about. I thought I was doing what a chair is supposed to do—bring problems to the attention of my colleagues. That had worked, and worked well, at UCSD. Meanwhile I was becoming a popular teacher, boosting enrollments, forging links with some interdisciplinary programs (Women and Gender Studies, American Studies), raising money. But every step I took seemed only to further aggravate my Macalester colleagues.

I knew things were careening out of control one April morning, unusually cold even for Minnesota, when one of the department's associate professors and I pulled into the parking lot at the same time. I smiled in his direction, but he would not look at me, even to nod. It was a small thing, insignificant in itself, but, as Joyce Carol Oates describes them, one of those tiny moments that signals that something momentous and unexpected is happening, that your life is about to change for the worse, that a disaster is underway. A colleague does not meet your gaze in the parking lot, does not acknowledge your existence. A simple moment that could have any number of explanations—he was preoccupied, thinking about the class he was about to teach. He was distracted. He didn't see me.

But he had seen me, and would not look at me. My body, stomach clenching, knew, right then, I was in serious trouble.

Later, I tried again to imagine how things looked from my colleagues' points of view. I was an outsider, but had quickly been made chair. The department had been operating one way, and then I quickly made changes (those damn voting rules). They had settled on a given set of requirements, worked hard on those courses, and I raised questions about requiring them. But instead of forthrightly disagreeing or seeking compromise, my colleagues attacked, and, after attacking, chose the nuclear option.

What the hell is going on?

I asked in my journal, and I really had no idea. Nothing that had happened seemed to me to be beyond the boundaries of normal academic give and take, and in fact the substantive disagreements seemed quite ordinary by UCSD standards. And yet my colleagues went behind my back to the Provost, which even Chuck, my retiring colleague—who never said a bad word about anybody—called unconscionable.

The Provost then added gasoline to the fire. He had promised to let me tell my side of the story, at a brief meeting to which I brought Chuck for support. He spoke to everyone in the department and then summoned me to his office again, alone, for another meeting, at which I expected to explain what was happening as I saw it. I had talking points ready (*well, you did choose to make me chair soon after arriving, in retrospect, that was a mistake, no one was ready for it—and they should have realized what I could and could not teach*), and I even dressed up for the occasion. But instead of letting me say more than a word or two, he removed me as chair.

Suddenly I was Kate in *Mary of Scotland*, about to be executed. And here all along I thought I was Hepburn in *Pat and Mike*, a champion. We had one substantive exchange:

Provost: *Your colleagues feel they can't talk to you about the curriculum.*

Me: *I've held a series of meeting specifically to talk about the curriculum.*

It felt like English had suddenly become a language I no longer understood.

I was at a complete loss, and my law genes were kicking in. Didn't I deserve at least a smidgen of due process? *A chance to speak?* Wasn't he interested in my side of the story? What, exactly, had I done that required impeachment? I didn't really care about being chair—been there, done that—but I was furious at the way I was being treated.

The Provost's mind was made up. He had no interest in hearing anything further from me.

It was not a pretty scene. I told him he was not honoring his commitment to hear me out and mentioned a lawyer. He threw me out of his office. I did in fact consult an attorney, but that was a waste of time, since no laws had been broken. I still had a job and a salary.

I tried going above the Provost's head. Both Chuck and I wrote to the President to point out that I had been promised, and then denied, a hearing, but the President refused to intervene. The President, of course, was Brian Rosenberg.

Never have I better understood the nostrum that no good deed goes unpunished.

By this point in the conflict, all of my genes—my law genes, my gay saboteur genes—were churning in overdrive. They should have known what they were getting when they hired me, I told myself; I certainly had a long enough record to examine. And I was not going to turn myself into something I wasn't, which, interestingly enough, had also been part of the dynamic in that earlier, difficult tenure case. That young woman was hired and then expected magically to become something *she* wasn't. It was assumed both of us would somehow transform into practitioners of mainstream, empirical political science, which neither of us were or wanted to be.

Apples can't turn themselves into pineapples, and it's ridiculous to expect them to, and especially ridiculous to beat up an apple for being an apple after buying it and taking it home from the supermarket.

More to the point, this was not the way professionals, or grown-ups, behaved.

I had never experienced colleagues this quick to go ballistic, or dealt with administrators this high-handed. Coming soon after the presidential search, the experience left me agreeing with Mary Cantwell: academics were people with more brains than sense. The whole place was beginning to feel like a loony bin.

I was upset and in a panic: What do I do *now*?

I was removed as chair in April. The summer passed in a haze, equal parts depression and fury. There were weeks when I couldn't eat or sleep much at all, then weeks of too much of both. Even Patsy knew something was wrong that summer. During the depressive phase she would stay very close, not spend much time out in the yard, put her head in my lap even more than usual. Then when I stormed around the house in a fury, she hid in the guest room and would only come to her bed in a corner of my room after I was asleep.

When school started up again, it was the only September I have ever not loved; I dreaded going to the office. I was tense and so was everyone else, as we all went about our daily business with eyes averted. The new chair, one of the associate professors who had gone behind my back to the Provost, tried to smooth things over by holding a party, inviting everyone.

Never have I less wanted to go to a social event. I drove around and around St. Paul on my way there, telling myself I needed to show up for at least half an hour. I gritted my teeth and finally showed up, quite late. I brought a cheap bottle of wine, and when I arrived I could see muscles and faces tighten up. I spoke mostly to spouses.

Then the Provost arranged for us all to meet with an outside facilitator, but at the same time forbade any discussion of what had happened—we were only to discuss how we would do business going forward, which seemed a bit like asking a pathologist to do an autopsy without the body.

Everyone made nice in front of the facilitator. The knives that had come out of hiding just a few months prior were nowhere to be found, and, given the Provost's rules, I couldn't point to the bloody footprints on the carpet. I wasn't sure which was worse, the tight, false smiles at the new chair's party or the pledges of cooperation at the facilitation.

One social event and one content-free meeting with an outsider were not going to be enough, at least not for me. I couldn't fathom it— hiring a senior scholar into an endowed chair—the most prestigious chair at Macalester, I was told—and then treating him the way I had been treated. Yes, perhaps I rushed in too quickly as chair, but was a disagreement about the curriculum, or anything else, really worth all this drama, all this back-stabbing?

For a long time I struggled to come up with an explanation for all the drama I was experiencing, both at Macalester and in my next job. It felt like I was being slapped around at these small colleges, and I didn't understand why, or what I had done to bring on so much combat. I couldn't comprehend why the atmosphere was so different from the universities where I had studied and taught, why the people around me were behaving the way they were—so unconscionably, as my senior colleague at Macalester had put it.

As with most political phenomena, I eventually saw psychology as key. I assembled in my head a profile for small college faculty and administrators.

Many at a small college look inward, to the institution, for their sense of self, much more so than at large universities, and some then become over-attached to having things go their way. Egos are heavily invested, easily bruised, and require care and feeding. At large universities, or at least the ones with which I was familiar, one usually never gave a moment's thought to one's colleagues' feelings about any matter of business. If you disagreed about something, you said so. If an argument followed, so be it. There were colleagues at UCSD with whom I seldom agreed about anything important in fourteen years, yet our relations outside of department meetings and discussions of business were never less than cordial. I observed the same pattern at Harvard. Business was business, disagreement was expected, votes were taken. It was never personal.

At a small college, everything is personal.

In addition, a fair number of senior faculty at small colleges are rather worn out from trying to maintain a professional profile while teaching a heavy load, and at the same time are frustrated about not having made it to the top of the heap in academia, which (they imagine) would mean a prestigious university appointment. As time goes on, they compare themselves to their peers who do have such appointments, and they think they are just as good—which is often true. Luck and serendipity have a great deal to do with who ends up where. Some then feel stuck, and compensate. Since the phone never rang from Berkeley or Columbia or the University of Chicago, they say to themselves, perhaps only semi-consciously, if I have to stay here, I'm going to whip this small department/program/college into shape, be a big fish in a small pond.

All of this sounds logical and somewhat obvious—now—but it took a long time to puzzle it out. I had found myself swimming in small ponds surrounded by sharks (and shark wannabes), some with very sharp teeth, and my previous experience at large universities left me ill prepared for the experience. I knew how to stand my ground—an essential skill in my previous jobs—but that only made people angrier.

I had solved one problem—my unhappiness with the research mania of large, ambitious universities—but replaced it with another—enough small college colleagues and administrators without scruples, more than willing to fight dirty.

As the saying goes, you pays your money, you takes your choice.

As someone who thought about rules, fairness, and due process on an almost daily basis—it was the core of my academic subject—I was headed for trouble. I didn't realize that different leagues have different rules. And I was senior now. Perhaps naively, I expected not only fairness, but perhaps even a bit of deference, certainly treatment like an equal, a peer. Due process, which anyone, junior or senior, deserved.

Was I expecting too much? Was I playing Julia in *Notting Hill*—a STAR—when I should have been playing her in *Steel Magnolias*—the member of an ensemble, one of many, letting Shirley MacLaine and Olympia Dukakis have the best scenes?

I can only say how it felt. I thought I was diligently following the script handed to me, playing the parts I had been hired to play. And then, doing my best in each role, it felt way too much like I was suddenly thrust into a different movie—*The Pelican Brief*, where people really did want to rub Julia out.

Reluctantly, I concluded there was nothing to be done after the blowup at Macalester but to go back out onto the job market. I really didn't want to; it felt like I had just gotten settled. I wasn't even finished fixing up my house. But I couldn't imagine working for years in such a small dysfunctional place, risking another bloodletting every time there was a serious disagreement.

I'm not suited to playing the black sheep,

I wrote in my journal. I decided I had no choice but to find a different pasture.

So Miss Julia jumped out of the frying pan.

And landed in the fire.

Oberlin College was looking for a Dean. Oberlin had more stature in the academic world than Macalester; it produced more students who went on to receive PhDs than any other undergraduate institution. A long line of distinguished political scientists, including three of my UCSD colleagues, had been students there. I had applied to Oberlin as an undergraduate and had almost gone.

True, Oberlin was in a small town in Ohio, but then, as Julia learned in *Duplicity*, life is full of difficult choices.

I had visited Oberlin in 1993 at the invitation of Ron Kahn. My second book had just been published, and Ron was using it in a course; he invited me to lecture. So during the last weekend in April, I attended the LGBT March on Washington, reconnecting with many of my East Coast friends, then on Monday flew to Ohio. My lecture was scheduled for the evening.

I assumed that, like most such events, there would be twenty students there, tops.

There were over sixty, and I was floored by how many had read my book carefully and by the really smart, probing questions. It was exhilarating.

The seed that had gotten planted at my Bard interview was beginning to grow.

Tensions remained high in my department at Macalester. We had another hire to make. I was not at all impressed with the person some of the others wanted to hire, and was able to persuade (in open meetings) enough outside members of the search committee—faculty from other departments, students—to vote against him. One of my colleagues, furious, came to my office after the vote and told me that "a day of reckoning is coming."

Apparently he thought he was Gary Cooper in *High Noon*, but I wasn't in that movie. That was Grace Kelly, well before Miss Julia's time.

I was fifty-three. An academic loses the ability to move by fifty-five or fifty-six, or so said the conventional wisdom at the time. I swallowed hard and applied to Oberlin.

* * *

Early interview, a hotel room at the Cleveland airport. Seemed to go well. Two-day interview on campus, exhausting.

Waiting. The search committee sends two members to Macalester to talk to people, to check me out. They allow me to give them a list of people to whom they should not speak. Still, I feel creepy, knowing they are on campus asking who knows who, who knows what.

More waiting.

The phone call comes. It's a Sunday, I've just gotten home from eating an omelet at my local hangout when the phone rings, and when I see the caller ID showing "Oberlin College" I know I got the job. Otherwise they wouldn't call on a Sunday.

Now I must go through their tenure process, must be vetted academically yet again. Send them syllabi, teaching evaluations, copies of my books.

More waiting.

Tenure is granted.

I visit again with the offer pending, talk to various people, lunch with the Politics department, dinner at the President's house. It's mid-May, perfect weather, the trees blooming though still bare in Minnesota.

List the St. Paul house, find a place to live in Oberlin—a sublet for the summer above the town's one movie theatre. Buy a house, into which I cannot move until August. There is no time, I look at only one house, it will do nicely. It's lovely, in fact. Too big but it's available. Take it.

Call the movers. Pack. Everything rushed, chaotic. "Am I really moving again?" I ask a friend one evening as he drinks tea and I sit at the dining room table making lists.

Yes, Julia is moving—bolting, just like in *The Runaway Bride*.

Drop the dog at my sister's house in Northern Illinois, can't have her in the sublet. Drive to Oberlin. Start over.

Yet again.

* * *

H. N. Hirsch served as Dean of the Faculty of Arts and Sciences at Oberlin College from July 1, 2005 until September 6, 2006, when he resigned.

Version A: Hirsch walked into an impossible situation. A controversial strategic plan had just been passed calling for the elimination of seven faculty positions. That's a large number at a small institution, and no dean could succeed if forced to begin his term by eliminating faculty slots. Tensions were high. Everyone was worried about losing a position.

Version B: Hirsch failed to establish a working relationship with the College President.

Version C: The President under whom Hirsch worked had lost the respect and confidence of many members of the faculty. A new dean from outside the institution couldn't possibly succeed in that kind of situation.

Version D: Being a dean at a small college is herding cats. Faculty members are not trained to be cooperative or to compromise. They are trained to believe there is a Right Answer, and that they are smart enough to find it. This is especially true at Oberlin, which prides itself on its rigor. That is a recipe for conflict, and there was plenty.

Verson E: Hirsch was a lousy dean. He was wrong for the job. His skin was much too thin.

Version F: Hirsch did as well as anyone could have done under impossible conditions.

Version G: Neither party talked, so who knows what really happened.

Version H: Hirsch's resignation came later on the same day a petition signed by almost seventy tenured members of the College faculty was delivered to the Board of Trustees, asking that the President be replaced. That can't be a coincidence. Finding herself in serious trouble with the faculty, the President tried to change the subject, or was lashing out.

Version I: Hirsch was a lunatic, unfit for the job. How he got chosen is beyond comprehension. He was way too pushy (like Julia in *Charlie Wilson's War*).

Version J: Hirsch's problem was ambivalence (like Julia in *My Best Friend's Wedding*). He wasn't sure he liked the job, and ended up wanting out.

Version K: Hirsch studied politics, taught constitutional law. He cared about procedure. He was willing to back decisions made by College committees even when he disagreed with the outcome. The President didn't care about procedure and wanted specific outcomes. They were on different wavelengths.

Version L: Poor Harry. He spent most of his career at large universities. He just didn't understand.

Version M: The President overruled decisions she didn't like, and that created problems—with Hirsch and with faculty committees, especially after a decision had been made public. The Oberlin faculty really does believe in faculty governance.

Version N: There is a structural problem at Oberlin; resources are spread too thin. No dean can be a success when forced to say "no" so often.

Version O: Hirsch walked into a civil war. He had to choose sides.

Version P: All of the above.

Version Q: None of the above.

Version R: Some of the above.

* * *

Here is what I remember.

I remember how glad I was to finish my first year as Dean, how glad I was that a new school year was beginning and I would know what to expect.

I was wrong. I didn't know what to expect.

I remember that on the Friday afternoon before the Labor Day weekend, at the beginning of what was to be my second year as Dean, my staff assistant told me that the President's office had just called and the President wanted to see me on Tuesday morning, the day after Labor Day, the first day of classes. We normally met on Mondays, but since Monday was Labor Day we were going to skip our weekly meeting, as we usually did if there was a holiday or she was out of town.

The meeting Tuesday morning was then switched to Wednesday afternoon at 2:30, my assistant told me just about an hour later on that Friday afternoon. I realized it was changed to Wednesday afternoon so it would take place after the first faculty meeting of the year at noon on Wednesday, where, as was the custom, the Dean would be called upon to introduce new members of the faculty.

I remember that when my assistant told me, on the Friday before Labor Day, that the meeting with the President had quickly been changed from Tuesday morning to Wednesday afternoon, I knew that trouble was coming, another one of those moments, something unimportant in and of itself, something slightly out of the ordinary, and you know, you somehow know in the pit of your stomach that your world is about to change.

I remember that I did very little over the holiday weekend, except that on Saturday evening I briefly saw Lisa Anderson, who had been my colleague at Harvard and was now at Columbia, who was dropping off her son for his last year at Oberlin. I remember thinking we were getting old, Lisa and I, that I knew her early in her marriage before she had children, before either of us had grey hair.

Seeing Lisa reminded me that life has chapters.

I remember that after I finally came to blows with the President on Wednesday at 2:30, I felt very calm—that Lillian Hellman kind of calm, again. I walked down to my office and handed a folder to the two associate deans, telling them about a phone call that needed to be made that afternoon about a pending hire. I said goodbye to the rest of the staff and left the building. I remember the astonished looks on everyone's face.

On the short ride home I remembered that one of the staff members who had been around the longest had warned me, soon after I arrived:

There are people who want you to fail.

That night, at home, I watched myself in *Notting Hill* and ordered pizza.

I remember that on the Sunday following Labor Day, after reading the *New York Times* and eating waffles, as I usually did on Sunday mornings, I went to the office to pack my personal belongings.

There was at the time an active faculty list-serve at Oberlin, and I remember that all that week, while I slept or watched movies, people said nice things about me on the list-serve and discussed the need to confront the President.

And then:

On Monday, a week after Labor Day, the day after I cleaned out my office, five days after I resigned as dean, the President announced she would be leaving in June.

I remember that one could almost feel a change in the barometric pressure.

The next day, Tuesday, one of the faculty members who wanted the President gone told me that I was collateral damage.

Wikipedia: *"Collateral damage is damage to things that are incidental to the intended target. It is frequently used as a military term where non-combatants are accidentally or unintentionally killed or wounded and/or non-combatant property damaged as result of the attack on legitimate military targets."*

I remember that the next few months passed in a fog, and that Patsy, my retriever, suddenly began losing weight and became seriously ill, as if she knew what was happening and tried to absorb the stress for me.

Patsy recovered quickly. It took me longer. I began to recover in the spring, when I was happy, near-deliriously happy, to be back in the classroom.

And I remember, most of all, thinking that students were undoubtedly the sanest constituency at a liberal arts college.

9
GAY STUDIES

I was a junior in high school at the time of the Stonewall rebellion in 1969. Like many of similar age and inclination, I suspect, I knew deep down that Stonewall had something to do with me, but did not know what.

Over the four decades since then, I have watched and participated in a remarkable social phenomenon—the queering of American academia.

Today's situation would be virtually unimaginable to an LGBT student or academician before Stonewall. Many, perhaps the majority of American colleges and universities have courses with queer content. Scholarship about sexuality has exploded, and queer ideas, such as Judith Butler's theories about the artificiality of gender, have found a permanent place in the humanities. On some progressive campuses, the queer student association is one of the largest groups, and the annual drag ball is a major event, as it has been at Oberlin. Some students arrive at college now proudly and loudly proclaiming their queerness, or at least ready to explore it. At Oberlin many are willing in class to discuss their own sexuality with breathtaking matter-of-factness, a matter-of-factness that sometimes leaves my head spinning. Not long ago, during a discussion of Catharine MacKinnon's theories of male domination, a young woman, much taken with MacKinnon's ideas, threw up her hands and said, "I just, I just, I just don't see why anyone would want a penis."

For the first time in three decades of teaching, I was speechless. Luckily one of the gay men in the class came to my rescue. "I'll explain it to you after class," he said to the young woman, and everyone chuckled.

So the current generation of students, or at least a segment of them—those lucky enough to figure themselves out early, those not overly influenced by evangelical religion, perhaps—seem extraordinarily comfortable with sexuality and with queer sexuality.

But what about the professoriate? Many of our students may be open, accepting, and nonchalant, but what about our colleagues?

Within the last few years several incidents have led me to ask: How much have things truly changed in the American academy? Are we really living in a world that much different from the bad old days before anyone came out? Are we accepted, or merely tolerated, and what's the difference? Are we still, on some level, treated as second-class citizens? Are queer subjects in the curriculum truly welcomed?

I have come to some distressing conclusions about these questions. I am, of course, but one American academic, of a certain age, in one conservative discipline, who has lived a particular life—institution X at time Y under conditions Z. Whether my experience speaks to a general situation—a condition—is a question I cannot answer.

Incident #1. Just as there are now openly queer faculty and students on many campuses, there are faculty who are not happy with this state of affairs, and say so. There are those who continue to believe that states should criminalize sodomy—for centuries the chief legal tool brandished against same-sex intimacy—and those who believe that the only legitimate sexual expression is within heterosexual marriage. Some of these faculty make these views known through their writing and public utterances.

One such scholar has been Robert George, Walter Murphy's successor as McCormick Professor of Jurisprudence at Princeton. I know Professor George, but not well. He organized a conference some years ago and kindly included me in the event and included my essay for the conference (on free speech, ironically) in the volume of essays resulting from the conference.

Some time later, David Brooks wrote a column in the *New York Times* praising Professor George and other conservative faculty for their courage in bucking the trend of what Brooks sees as today's politically correct campus culture.

In response to the Brooks column, Dan Pinello, a gay faculty member at City University of New York, posted a comment on the Lawcourts list-serve, an electronic discussion forum of scholars with an interest in law. Pinello took issue with Brooks, and talked about the harm done by Professor George to LGBT students exposed to George's views in the classroom.

In response to Pinello, Walter Murphy posted a message making it clear that he was annoyed with Pinello and with the suggestion that George might in any way be causing harm. Murphy praised George for having the courage to press against orthodoxy, and talked about how useful it was to have such iconoclasts presenting their ideas in the academy.

I was surprised by Walter's post. I knew him to be a man of honor, was taken aback by his tone of annoyance, and thought he was missing the point. The issue wasn't Professor George's right to say what he thought. Most everyone would argue in favor of that. The issue was whether such devotion to Professor George's freedom to say what he likes comes at a high price, as it also could cause genuine harm, harm that should in some way be taken seriously. College students, after all, can be particularly vulnerable or confused about their sexual orientation, and see faculty members as important authority figures. More than a knee-jerk defense of unpopular ideas was required.

So I said this in my own post to the list. I did not hesitate to answer Walter, despite his place in my life, and the profession, as a highly respected authority figure. I knew he believed in intellectual give and take.

The "idea" that sodomy should be illegal, I said, wasn't quite in the same category as the idea that taxes were too high or that the war in Iraq was a mistake. It was an "idea" that challenged the fundamental civil rights of a segment of the population, including some of Professor George's students, and perhaps that challenged not just what they *thought,* but their right *to be.* "Gay sex should be criminalized" is not quite the same kind of statement as "taxes are too high," I argued. It's much more personal. It could hit an eighteen- or twenty-year-old in the gut. I referred to Professor George's public stand on LGBT issues as homophobic, a characterization I'd describe as self-evident, although he and his defenders vigorously disagree with that characterization.

The battle was joined. Walter and I tussled back and forth, first on the public list, and then through private emails. In these emails, I described my own experience at Princeton in the mid-1970s, where I found the climate decidedly chilly on these questions. Thirty years had passed, and, I assumed, Walter would surely know how much things had changed in the interim, how much they needed to change.

What interests me for present purposes is not the question of which one of us is right about Professor George, about homophobia, or about Princeton. What astounded me during our exchange, and what astounds me still, was the degree of anger Walter displayed toward me, in part, it seemed, for using the word "homophobia" to describe George's opinion that same-sex intimacy should be, ought to be, criminalized. Walter all but ended our relationship, a relationship that, while not close, had been nothing but pleasant for many years. "You remind me of a child having a tantrum," he wrote. The last of my email messages to him came back with this note: "Returned unread." A few months later, at Christmas, I wrote him a letter, but it was never answered.

Apparently, Professor George had a right to believe, and say, that sodomy should be illegal and that only heterosexual marriage should be honored, but, as a gay man, I did not have the equivalent right, in Walter's mind, to call this homophobia, or to point out that the expression of such views might raise difficulties for LGBT students, or to describe my own experiences.

Incident #2. That job interview at Bard College. I meet with the College's President. The students love him, refer to him by his first name. The conversation evolves in a manner in which I need to come out as gay.

I do.

At first, he seems to take it in stride. He then brings up AIDS. This is 1987, the height of the crisis. He says he considers himself just as vulnerable to the disease as I.

I appreciate his saying that.

He then says, "If you were to become ill, you would need to step away, to protect the institution."

Step away.

Does he realize, I wonder, this learned and accomplished and no doubt liberal man, that he was saying I would need to "step away" from health insurance?

He talks on, changing the subject, but I am no longer listening; I know I would not accept the job if offered.

As he talks I am thinking of my friend Carl in Boston, between jobs when diagnosed, and so without health insurance. I am thinking of the night I stayed with him until 3:00 a.m. as he sobbed that he didn't know what he would do. He fell asleep, finally, and I dozed in a chair, and in the morning we went out for breakfast.

Six months later he was dead.

Incident #3. The setting: I call one of those fateful meetings of my colleagues at Macalester to talk about the curriculum. The meeting quickly becomes tense, and, to my surprise, my colleagues want to talk about my courses, when the topic up for discussion is our sequence of introductory courses. It turned out that my colleagues were not happy with some of the courses I had been teaching—especially "Gender, Sexuality, and the Law" and a course called "The Politics of Sexual Minority Communities," both of which were courses I had talked about wanting to teach when I was interviewed for the position. I was not pulling my weight, it seems. I was not doing my job. "You were hired to teach AMERICAN politics," one colleague thundered at me, and others then piled on.

What's relevant here is the implicit assumption that any course touching on the politics of gender or sexuality was not, could not be, considered American politics—despite the fact that all of the material in these courses concerned the United States. In "Gender, Sexuality, and the Law," ninety-seven percent of what we read was American case law and supporting historical and theoretical material. In "The Politics of Sexual Minority Communities" we covered the history and politics of LGBT communities in the United States (and only the United States) from the early twentieth century to the present. But somehow the fact that these courses concerned gender and sexuality, covered LGBT subjects, made them, literally, un-American—suspect, foreign, less worthy. By teaching them, I was not contributing to the College, I was letting down the home team. Attacking these courses because of their content—one colleague called them "boutique courses"—a word which, arguably, carries a sexual tinge—was fair game. Real men wouldn't be caught dead in a boutique, would they?

Incident #4. In the fall of 2007, I was elected to the executive council of the American Political Science Association. Soon after that, a controversy erupted over the site of the 2012 annual meeting of the Association. Back in the early 1990s, the LGBT Caucus asked for a change in the Association's convention siting policy. We asked that the Association commit itself not to meet in any city that violates the civil rights of its members, including its LGBT members, some of whom traveled with their partners or children to the annual meeting. Given that queer sex was still illegal in some of these locations, this was an important matter. We felt the Association could not ask its members to put themselves in any degree of legal jeopardy, or to choose between their families and their professional obligations.

At the time, most members of the Caucus were willing to accept a compromise focusing on local policy. That is, if a particular city had non-discrimination legislation, we were willing to overlook the fact that the state in question still had on its books a sodomy law. In most states, such state sodomy laws were seldom enforced.

This legal situation changed dramatically in the first years of the twenty-first century, when, in a stunning and unexpected move, the United States Supreme Court in 2003 declared unconstitutional all remaining state sodomy laws, overturning *Bowers v. Hardwick*. Then, one year later, the highest court in Massachusetts allowed same-sex marriages in that state, thus beginning the same-sex marriage movement.

There was, of course, a political backlash against these developments. Many states quickly adopted new laws or amended their state constitutions to say that "marriage" could only apply to a man and a woman. Some states went even further than that, declaring that no member of a same-sex couple could enjoy the "incidents" of marriage—all the rights and privileges that go along with the legal status.

These "incident" clauses were very serious. In effect, they declared that the state in question would not recognize a marriage, a registered domestic partnership, or a civil union between two men or two women legally valid in another state. Arguably, they also prevented the recognition of a private agreement covering a matter such as medical power of attorney—the right to make medical decisions or visit in a hospital—in the case of an emergency, and thus raised questions of safety for LGBT couples and families traveling to the state.

As a result of these new draconian and homophobic state laws, some LGBT members of the APSA asked the Association to move its 2012 meeting out of New Orleans. The state of Louisiana had in fact adopted one of the most egregiously discriminatory of these new constitutional amendments.

A long, painful, and somewhat dirty battle on the APSA Council ensued. Given that the Association had already committed itself not to meet in locations that violated the civil rights of its members, and given the harshness of the Louisiana law, a conclusion seemed obvious: We could not meet in New Orleans, despite that city's reputation as a happy tourist destination for all.

But after exhaustive maneuvering, the Council voted to stay in New Orleans. What's particularly relevant here is not that our demand was not met, but rather the degree to which it was treated, by some, as illegitimate—as the crazy, hysterical demand of a bizarre fringe group trying to take over the Association. What was also remarkable was the degree to which our arguments were met with sloppy thinking.

We asked, "If a state said that marriages between Jews and non-Jews were invalid, would the Association meet there?" We were told the analogy did not hold. Why not, we asked? Well, LGBT issues are "in flux," and should not be "frozen" at any particular point, a distinguished political scientist, an officer of the Association, intoned.

What, exactly, was in flux, one wondered. Our right to form intimate associations and families? Our right to have such associations recognized in an emergency? We pointed to the tragic case of a woman denied access to her dying partner in a hospital in Miami—another Southern city with a reputation as gay-friendly. The women lived in Washington State, where they had registered as domestic partners. They traveled to Miami with their two children; in Miami, one of them had a severe stroke.

At the hospital, her partner was unceremoniously told "this is an anti-gay state," and both she and the children were denied access to the stricken spouse. "What if this happens to a political scientist at the convention in New Orleans?" we asked. The women in Miami had legal papers of various kinds, including a medical power of attorney, sent to the hospital in question, all to no avail.

"We don't know if the same thing would happen in New Orleans," we were told. "Well," we replied, "over seventy percent of the people of

Louisiana voted for this constitutional amendment, isn't that a little scary?" "You need real evidence," we were told.

At one point, another queer colleague and I were assigned to a sub-committee of the Council charged with coming up with a proposal for dealing with the situation. Another member of the subcommittee—yet another distinguished political scientist, and again someone I had known for many years—early on said we shouldn't do much of any-thing, and then raised questions about the presence of queer members on the committee. People had "concerns" about anyone with a clear position on the issue, a member of the affected group, being on the committee, this colleague said. Arguing that the committee should be quite circumspect, he noted that "people have concerns about the com-mittee's legitimacy."

This was stunning. It is unimaginable that the APSA, or any aca-demic association, would create a committee to deal with an issue touching any other minority group—African Americans, Latinos, Jews, women—without representation from the group in question. But somehow we were different—the presence of openly LGBT members of the profession on the committee raised "questions." At a minimum, it seemed, these comments were meant to silence us, or to delegitimate anything we might say—before we had a chance to say it. I resigned from the committee, and, for a time, the committee's work was sus-pended. It was, however, later revived and given an important task, but the member's comments—which the (non-gay, non-queer) chair of the committee (whom I had never before met) described as creating a "toxic" atmosphere—were never addressed.

During its long consideration of this issue, the Association asked for input from its membership, and opinion was almost evenly split. What was eye opening, however, was the number of political scientists who referred to the proposal to pull out of New Orleans in derogatory terms—"politically correct nonsense"; "silly"; "absurd." "Let me put it delicately," one member wrote into the special website set up to take member comments. "You guys have run amok." Several said they would quit the Association if the conference was moved.

To be sure, many members treated our concerns seriously, and many wanted to keep the conference in New Orleans as a means of expressing solidarity with the city—and its large minority population—in the wake of Hurricane Katrina. We tried to argue that there were many ways of helping the city other than scheduling a conference there seven years after the disaster. I have no quarrel with those who believe the issue presented a tough choice—who recognized the valid arguments on each side, and came down in favor of staying in New Orleans. What brought me up short was the degree to which the argument to leave New Orleans, and those making the argument, were treated with derision.

Incident #5. I was, twice, considered for a position at Johns Hopkins University. A senior person there was a fan of my work and kindly wrote letters of recommendation when I needed them. In the first round of job negotiations, he vigorously urged me to join his department without tenure. But this was right after my book on Frankfurter was published, and I demurred. I still had years left on my Harvard contract and, with a book out making something of a splash, I was hoping when I moved to move with tenure. That was how to win the Harvard game.

The second time I was considered was later, after I had moved to UCSD. No offer came, and I didn't think much of it at the time—no big deal. It happens.

Years later, I am chatting with a member of the Hopkins department at a conference, and I ask him, out of curiosity, what happened the second time.

It was my erstwhile supporter who torpedoed me, he tells me. "He said you were damaged goods."

Damaged goods. Not "I wasn't as impressed with his second book as his first book," but *damaged goods*.

I am stunned.

I discuss his comment, as reported to me, with a former Harvard colleague.

"What changed?" I wonder.

"You came out. You organized that gay panel. Everyone noticed."

I stare at him.

"What's he like, this guy?" my friend asks.

"A Southern gentleman."

My friend smiles.

His explanation is, at best, a working hypothesis. But it never even occurred to me.

"Wake up, Harry," my friend advises.

Incident #6. I have just arrived at Oberlin, where I have been named Dean of the Faculty of Arts and Sciences. I am having lunch at a local restaurant, and I hear a conversation in another booth about me. I am referred to as "that faggot." There is much laughter. "It shouldn't be too hard to get rid of that faggot."

I do not know who is speaking, I cannot see him, and I don't want to. I stop eating, ask for my bill, and leave.

* * *

So what sort of impression do these incidents make? What do they tell us about the place of a gay educator in the early years of the new century?

The first thing I should note is the profound impact these incidents had on me. Each one of them produced shock, the kind of shock described by anthropologist Esther Newton in her discussion of her own academic career, the kind of shock that, if one is not careful, can lead to a "bitterness that can trap you in a perpetual dance with the limits straight society sets." Newton also perceptively points out that homophobia in the academy often comes neatly packaged. "Homophobia in the academic world is not the violent shove in the back," Newton writes. "It occurs in a privileged context where hostility is rarely so crudely expressed. But," she cautions, such genteel homophobia "does break spirits, damage careers, ruin lives."

Did these incidents break my spirit? For a short time. As each of them first erupted in my life, the shock produced a kind of temporary paralysis—an inability to think or plan or react. I felt physically odd, as if I were on some kind of powerful new medication to which my body could not adjust.

After hearing myself described as "that faggot" at Oberlin just a few months after arriving—Oberlin, bastion of progressive, sometimes radical politics for 170 years, founded in the name of the abolition of slavery—I went straight home, called my office, told one of the secretaries I was not feeling well. I collapsed face-down on my bed, slept for hours, only got up when Patsy came and nudged me awake with her wet nose around 7:00 p.m. I ate cold spaghetti out of the refrigerator and collapsed again at 8:30, didn't get out of bed until 9:00 the next morning.

I had just moved into my house, everything was chaos, boxes half unpacked. I stared at the boxes for a long time. Finally I pulled out a random book: *Queer Studies*, an edited volume. I started laughing, so long and hard that Patsy grew alarmed. Over the next few days I went to the grocery store and had trouble focusing on the task at hand; what did I need in the kitchen? I put too much laundry soap in the washing machine and created a flood of suds on the basement floor.

After this and after each of these incidents, through some combination of orneriness and bravado, I forced myself to snap back, to reenter a normal state of being. But in each case a wound had been created, and there would be a scar, sometimes tiny, sometimes a huge gash.

Leaving Macalester wasn't a tragedy for me. I was strong enough to figure out I was being mistreated, and had enough of an academic record to land on my feet. I didn't lose my life or a limb or my livelihood, but it was certainly not what I had planned for myself at that stage of my life. I did have to give up a life I had worked hard to establish, and felt that I had wasted five years. Similarly, no one at the APSA would be so crude as to assault me or my queer colleagues physically, or even to insult us face to face, to say, "no, a bunch of faggots and dykes aren't going to force us to move the conference out of New Orleans," even if that's what they were thinking. Instead we were confronted with specious reasoning, with arguments that sounded at first glance sensible: "This issue is in flux." The result was profound bewilderment, not tragedy; alienation, to be sure, but not physical or lasting emotional damage. Walter Murphy called me no names, issued no threat. He just simply didn't want any more to do with me after I challenged him. I was no longer worthy of his time or attention. An important, if distant, relationship was lost. So the effect of all of these incidents on my life was serious, but not tragic. In some bizarre way, that represents progress.

Was I right to leave Macalester, to resign from the APSA committee? Should I have stayed and fought instead of withdrawing from the battle? In fact I did carry on the fight, and attempted in each case to shift it to a larger arena, where I hoped to find allies. At Macalester I wrote to the College President, and made clear that, at a minimum, intellectual homophobia was at play in the department—by which I meant a devaluing of any course with gay content—along with various other resentments and shenanigans. He quickly dismissed my claim.

One could argue that, under College policy, he had an obligation to investigate it, but no matter, apparently. He did not act. And at the APSA, I left the committee but, along with a wonderful LGBT colleague, fought hard on the larger Council and among the membership to get the conference moved out of New Orleans.

But it's also true that in each case, initially, my instinct was to flee, to leave town, to get the hell out of Dodge. And that leads me to wonder if these incidents had hit me at an earlier stage in my life and career whether the consequences would have been more profound, more lasting. Might I, in fact, have left the profession rather than simply left Macalester? Might Walter Murphy have prevented me from getting a job? He certainly had that power before I had established myself. How many young scholars face incidents like this and end up leaving their chosen fields of study?

When I look back, and ask myself whether these incidents carry any lessons extending beyond my own life and career, it's hard not to reach the conclusion that what they have in common is the expectation that queer faculty would be quiescent and silent: Seen and not heard. If we would make no real demands, if we said nothing about the condition of our queer students or colleagues, if we did not, God forbid, bring queerness into the classroom, if we did not in any way make life difficult or complicated for our straight colleagues, we would be admitted to the guild, shown the secret handshake. Our presence would be tolerated—we could be openly gay at Princeton, at Macalester, in the APSA—as we would not have been able to be in 1940 or 1950 or 1960. That is, in fact, progress. But bare tolerance, that passage just past the front door, would be all we could expect.

Without knowing it, I had struck a bargain in my professional life, and I am willing to guess it's a bargain struck by many still. I would be allowed to be openly gay so long as I did not make any real demands on mentors or colleagues or institutions. Yes, I had been told: You can come to the party. Just don't have more than one drink, and stand politely in the corner. Wear a conservative suit, and a tie.

And, for most of my career, I did. I got my PhD and worked hard. I chose a non-gay dissertation topic and got it published as a book. I taught well. Early on, I did not call attention to my sexual orientation. It was there, to be sure. Anyone with an ounce of awareness could figure it out. I just didn't call attention to it. I said nothing, did nothing, when a senior colleague at a Harvard faculty meeting, when I was an untenured assistant professor, made a homophobic slur and then looked straight at me. Security first, action later.

And that strategy worked. My books were published. I was granted tenure in a good department. I was promoted to full professor. And then, as it were, I came out of the professional closet. In a highly quantitative and professionally oriented department, I started teaching a course called "Gay and Lesbian Politics." A few eyebrows were raised. "You can't be serious," one well-meaning colleague at UCSD said to me. But I was; by then I had tenure, and I was safe. I was put on dissertation committees on queer subjects all over the University (the rules required an "outside" member on PhD committees). The Chancellor at the University where most of this first occurred even asked me to chair that committee he set up to open an LGBT activity office for students.

And I thought: Mission accomplished.

But I was wrong. True, these were all real signs of progress. But I was not being treated as an equal, at least as far as these gay-related activities were concerned. Somehow all of this work didn't really count. It was tolerated, to be sure—even parts of it encouraged by some, such as the Chancellor, for public relations purposes. But on some level it was not really valued. And so when push came to shove—as it did with Walter Murphy, as it did at Macalester, and as it did at the APSA—none of it really mattered. None of my decades of careful, polite, step by step movement inoculated me against what was coming.

As Toni McNaron has written of her time on the faculty at the University of Minnesota, I was living a professional life "threaded with ambiguity." Her academic career, she says, "simultaneously . . . nourished and assaulted me, gratified and punished me." McNaron, too, struck a bargain: "I am someone who could have 'played out' a butch identity," McNaron candidly writes, "if she had not wanted in the mid-1960s to be a professor of English in the Midwest." I wanted to be a professor of political science some twenty years later, and the terms of the contract remained the same.

And that leaves me now to wonder: What was the source of my timidity? And: What if I had been less careful?

No doubt temperament had something to do with my choices. I am not—or was not—by nature flamboyantly gay (my second grade teacher: *he's too quiet*). But what has become stunningly clear after three decades is that the chief source of my timidity, my early politeness, was my ambition. I wanted academic success, and the price at which that would come was crystal clear. I received my PhD in 1978. In the late Seventies and most of the Eighties, one did not become successful in political science by pursuing queer subjects, or by being a gay activist, even in one's private life. I accepted the bargain before I knew its terms, before I knew a negotiation was in progress. It was part of the air I breathed at Princeton and Harvard. I would work hard, and wait, and I would be rewarded.

And I was. Good schools. Good jobs. Reviews of my first book in the major venues. Tenure.

And then. And then I thought, well, I'm a senior member of the profession now, I can express my opinion about homophobia on a listserve. I can teach more courses with queer content. I can point out to the APSA that holding the convention in New Orleans violates an already-established policy.

And then I discovered the limits of tolerance, and I discovered the hypocrisy of conditional acceptance.

As political theorist Wendy Brown (as it happens, the colleague with whom I worked most closely on the APSA Council to move the annual meeting out of New Orleans) has brilliantly argued, "tolerance" is not equality; being tolerated is a second-class status. When one is tolerated, one carries a "marked" identity; the marking carries with it connotations of deviance, inferiority, and marginality. The subject who is tolerated is "identified as naturally and essentially different." By being tolerated, one's marginal status is "continuously inscribed." We are a threat, and we are seen as a threat when we make demands—even the demand to teach a particular course.

Wendy poses the key question: When an individual or group is tolerated, "what retreat from stronger ideals of justice is conveyed?" And the fact that tolerance persists over time leads Brown to ask, "what kind of fatalism about the persistence of hostile and irreconcilable differences in the body politic" does this demonstrate?

During the APSA controversy, Wendy and I continuously posed this question: If Louisiana or another state passed a law denying marriage or familial rights on the basis of race, or religion, or nationality, would we hesitate for a moment to move the conference out of that state? As Wendy succinctly put it to our colleagues, the law in Louisiana says to

LGBT citizens, "your partner is not your partner . . . your family is not your family." To a distinguished and learned group of political scientists, this did not provide a basis for action. Why? Because we are not in their eyes really equal. We'll be given jobs in the profession if we are openly queer, perhaps, if we're good enough at what we do; allowed on occasion to publish on LGBT subjects, at some institutions allowed to teach courses with LGBT content—but all on sufferance, not because we have a right to do so. We are being tolerated, and our relationships are seen as second class.

Perhaps this is not unusual for minority groups in the first stages of their emergence. McNaron thinks so; she argues that "from its inception this country has exacted a certain conformity in exchange for belonging." McNaron is quite right, I think, to point out this "fundamental hypocrisy," this "dangerous incongruence between ideals and practices." Perhaps I was naïve to think it could ever be otherwise.

So the price has been high. I feel a bit of what psychologists call buyer's remorse about my academic career.

But I also know that for those of us who have the stomach for it, the struggle is worth the price.

* * *

Graduation time at Oberlin. A student of mine is president of the senior class. She had taken four of my courses, and I supervised her honors thesis. She had been a queer activist on campus and a bit of a lightning rod. She wants to do graduate work in political theory and gender studies, and when Wendy and her partner—Judith Butler— bring their son Isaac, a senior in high school, to Oberlin to look it over, they ask me to find a student to show him around, and I ask this student. I introduce her to the famous theorists, and they ask her about her major. "I'm majoring in Harry," she said, and everyone laughed.

She refers to herself in her graduation speech as transgendered, and I watch some of the faces on the podium tighten ever so slightly as she speaks. The students cheer wildly when she is done.

As I listen to her speech, I remember. I remember all the years when I was closeted, the years when I was discreet, which is another form of being closeted. I think how long it took me to be open with myself, my colleagues, my students. I think how, when I was this student's age, no one was out, no one would have dared speak openly about queer sexuality, certainly not in a graduation speech.

No, not in a million years.

10
PSYCH 201

I have nothing to write about but myself, and this self that I have,
I hardly know of what it consists.

— Jean-Jacques Rousseau

I loved school.

There wasn't much else.

I never left.

I made myself into an intellectual, and then found out academic success was not the same thing.

Not the same thing at all.

I craved it—academic success—until I could no longer find it, or decided it wasn't worth it.

I do not know which.

I wanted to know the world.

I wanted to share what I knew.

I did.

I thought people in the academy would behave decently.

They did.

Later, some didn't.

A surprise.

I wanted to tell my story.

I do not know if my story is true.

I know only that it is mine.

I know one truth, now, at least. One truth about myself, my much younger self, something I can see after so many years.

I thought being smart was all that mattered.

You live in two harsh worlds, a therapist once said to me: The gay world, and academia.

She was right.

And she was wrong.

Harsh and fulfilling, nasty and nurturing, and inevitable. The only choices.

The only choices for me.

Late in her life, in an interview on German television, Hannah Arendt said, "No one really knows himself."

At times I'm sure she was right.

At times I'm sure she was wrong.

You come into this world, look around, make certain deductions, free yourself from the old bullshit, learn, think, observe, conclude.

— Julian Barnes

11

SOCIOLOGY 300
IMAGINING THE FUTURE

My academic field, constitutional law, is fond of using hypotheticals, which can be a useful tool both in scholarly writing and in the classroom ("suppose the President and Congress reinstitute the draft, and require eighteen-year-old men but not eighteen-year-old women to register. Would that be constitutional under current precedent?") And colleagues with whom I've discussed the topics and opinions I've covered here have often asked me, "So, how would you change things?"

These brief notes constitute my answer. If I could wave a magic wand, here is how I would remake American academia. As Dita Shklar once said to me, "Tell the truth as you see it, and to hell with everything else." As usual, she got straight to the point.

1. *The insane increase in tuition and the concomitant problem of student debt*

The federal government should institute a tuition remission program for both public and private institutions, in which every year of national service after graduation would be paid with the forgiveness of a specified amount of student debt as well as a nominal salary. The service could come in any form, including but not limited to the military, public school teaching, the provision of daycare services, the Peace Corps, and a domestic equivalent of the Peace Corps.

2. Academic tenure

It must be retained. Yes, Virginia, it is an essential guarantee of intellectual freedom, and benefits students in various ways. There is no way on earth I would have started teaching a course on gay politics, or become a gay activist within my discipline, without the protection of tenure.

The tenure clock, however—the number of years before you must apply for tenure—should be extended, for those who wish to extend it, up to twelve years. This will have two benefits: helping young families, and allowing faculty members at the beginning of their careers to spend more time and energy on their teaching.

3. PhD programs

No PhD program should continue to exist if it cannot reasonably place a set percentage of its graduates in full-time, well-salaried positions, inside or outside the academy, within three years of receiving their degree. Post-docs and adjunct teaching do not count. So that this does not hurt less popular fields, the required percentage should vary by discipline. A PhD program in political science, for example, could be required to place seventy percent of its graduates, classics perhaps forty percent, and so on. These numbers should be disclosed to new applicants.

4. Administration

Presidents, deans, and provosts should serve one term of specified length and then return to the faculty. The turnover will be healthy for these individuals as well as for the institutions they serve, and will prevent administrative arteriosclerosis. It will also prevent those with Napoleonic personality complexes from pursuing these positions.

5. Academic salaries and academic stars

Every institution should institute a ceiling on faculty salaries. No full professor should earn more than four times the salary of starting assistant professors (counting housing allowances). Every faculty member at every institution should be required to carry the same teaching load, with course reductions only for major administrative roles and major committee service.

6. *Adjuncts*

No more than twenty percent of courses at any institution should be taught by adjunct faculty. Adjunct appointments should be full-time and for a period of not less than two years, and carry full benefits and salaries not less than seventy-five percent of starting assistant professor salaries.

7. *First-year intensive writing*

What used to be called Freshman Comp should return, and be well-funded enough to employ enthusiastic and qualified teachers of writing. Every institution should also have a Writing Center which students can use voluntarily, or as directed by a faculty member.

8. *Student-faculty ratios*

No institution with a student-faculty ratio above 10:1 should be allowed to call itself a liberal arts college. States should require, and fund, a student-faculty ratio of 14:1 or better at its state-funded institutions.

Yes, Virginia, this will be expensive. Very expensive. It would require that we spend on higher education about twenty percent of what we currently spend on the military.

9. *The curriculum*

I can hear the gunfire now.

The current constellation of departments should be abolished in the undergraduate division, and all faculty members should be assigned to one of the following divisions, as outlined by Christopher Lucas:

Fine arts

Arts and letters

Social and humane studies

Physical sciences and technologies

Biological sciences and technologies

Students should be required to spend their first year broadly surveying each of these five areas.

10. *Team teaching should be encouraged and supported*

The need for team teaching came home to me in a major way when I began teaching American Political Thought at Macalester. In that course as traditionally taught, the material consists of primary documents—everything from the Mayflower Compact to the Port Huron Statement. We read the work of major figures such as Thoreau and Emerson, looked at the speeches of Jefferson and Lincoln, and so forth.

It makes absolutely no sense to study these texts apart from their historical context, or to exclude texts that are considered more literary and therefore not included, such as *Uncle Tom's Cabin*.

I find I need to spend a great deal of time in that course filling in the historical background of the texts and documents we read. Without that background, students are pretty much lost. For example, it is impossible to understand Thoreau without understanding the Mexican War, impossible to understand the Puritans without understanding political and religious conditions in England from which they fled, impossible to understand the Constitution without knowing something about economic conditions in the states after the Revolution.

By slicing off political theory and literature from history and economics, we are failing our students and creating generations of students who know next to nothing about the history of their country, or even basic facts about it.

When I arrived at UCSD I asked my first few classes, just for fun, to take what I called a literacy test. I asked them to answer questions such as these:

Name the states that border Illinois.

In what year did the Civil War start?

What is in the Fourth Amendment to the Constitution?

Name one American who has won the Nobel Prize.

I told them not to put their names on their papers. The results were horrifying.

Broad divisions in place of departments and team teaching will have the added benefit of reversing the ghettoization of fields allied to identity politics. The impulse to create programs in Ethnic Studies and Women and Gender Studies and similar programs over the last few decades has been an admirable impulse, but the result has been to create a parallel curriculum in small, separate departments and programs, and to leave larger departments and programs free to ignore these subjects—"oh, we don't have to hire anyone to do race, they do that in Ethnic Studies."

The faculty, in each division, should work together to determine what undergraduates need to know and how it should be taught. Political scientists need to work directly with historians, sociologists, philosophers, and so forth; biologists and chemists and specialists on the environment need to collaborate.

11. *Trustees*

There should be one faculty trustee and one student trustee for each twelve members of governing boards; they should have full voting power. Among other things, trustees set budgets, which control a great deal of what can and cannot happen on any given campus.

12. *Teaching*

Every institution should have a Center for Teaching, and every faculty member should be required to participate in one of its activities (which could include a reading group) at least once every six years. The quality of an individual's teaching should be judged not only by student evaluations but by peer observation as well.

13. *Rankings*

Congress should prohibit *U.S. News & World Report* and similar publications from publishing their rankings of institutions.

Yes, Virginia, this would be a violation of the First Amendment. As Emerson said, foolish consistency is the hobgoblin of little minds (and remember, this is all an exercise in fantasy).

The rankings have become an arms race, and are based in part on silly criteria, such as percent of alumni who donate money to the institution (not that money doesn't matter). Arms races are a form of collective insanity.

Epilogue:
September

On every campus, there are a few perfect days in late August or early September. The weather is the same, has been the same, whether it's Cambridge, Massachusetts or La Jolla, California, St. Paul, Minnesota or a small town in Ohio. It is perfect late summer weather, sunny, warm but not hot, cool breeze. It never rains. The consistency of the weather on these days in different parts of the country, over many years, is the only evidence I have ever had of the existence of a higher power.

The campus and town are suddenly crowded; the freshmen (now called "first years," perhaps out of excessive political correctness) are here with their parents. Boxes and suitcases are carried into dorms.

I walk around and watch them, and I remember the morning my father dropped me off in Ann Arbor so many years before.

The new students look anxious but do their best to hide it, some with exaggerated humor, some by showing irritation with their parents: they want them to be gone, for their new lives to begin. A few cling. The parents look proud and worried at the same time, the fathers more proud, the mothers, usually, more worried. More and more, now, there are two mothers or two fathers, something I thought I would not live to see. Younger siblings mill around, not knowing what to do with themselves.

I make it a point of going to the local dime store or drug store, where parents buy everything in sight, six cans of shaving cream or four different study lamps, so their kids will have enough supplies in their new life. I linger a while in the dime store or in the restaurant where I have lunch, catching snatches of conversation—"don't forget your asthma medicine"—and then I walk slowly across the campus. I drink it in. Sometimes I'm asked for directions, and a student or a parent starts a conversation: "what do you teach?" Then I watch tearful or joyous goodbyes, lots of hugging.

Later in the day I see students walking around in groups or two or three or four, getting acquainted with new roommates or suite-mates or people down the hall. One can already see signs of a few mismatched roommates: a punk rocker with a budding socialite, a tennis player in perfect whites with a barefoot hippie.

Oberlin has a music conservatory, so by late afternoon small groups are sitting on the grass listening to someone play an instrument or sing. I look into the faces of the first-year students, trying not to stare too long. Was I ever so young, I wonder? So full of promise, everything in front of me? I must have been, but it's far in the past now, it's hard to remember exactly how it felt. I am no longer one of them.

Instead I teach them, trying to nurture those who gravitate to me for one reason or another. Sometimes I will give advice, carefully, gingerly; sometimes it will be followed, sometimes not. Some will excel, some will surprise me, some will have a hard time.

After they graduate or years down the road, some will write me a note or letter, thanking me for a class or for advice or for being their advisor. Some will invite me to their wedding, send me Christmas cards, baby pictures. Two gay men met in my class in California, got together, got married when that was first briefly possible in that state, and adopted a little boy; their annual Christmas letter updates me on how their son is doing. Another former student, the son of a Methodist minister in North Carolina, every year sent me a "Happy New Year" card on the Jewish holidays, only it was the kind of New Year card one would send in January, with a drawing of a champagne glass or noise-makers; I never had the heart to correct him. I went to his funeral a few years ago, after he was killed by a drunk driver, hugged his wife and his daughter. Each fall I miss his cards.

It's a beautiful day so I linger and watch. The breeze feels wonderful and someone is playing the flute. Finally, reluctantly, I go home, work on my syllabus, prepare the first class, answer my email.

Next week or next month or later in the fall, there will be a cold rain, I will feel frazzled, I will teach an occasional lackluster class, some students will mess up in one way or another, and I will wonder what I am doing, what difference any of it makes. But not yet. Not today.

Today I can imagine no other life.

References

Page   Source

3   **Radical:** Kalle Lasn, "Cultural Jamming," in *The Radical Reader*, ed. Timothy Patrick McCarthy and John McMillan (New York: The New Press, 2003), 633.

13   **Doris Lessing**: *Walking in the Shade: 1949 to 1962* (New York: Harper Collins, 1997), 62.

32   **The me decade**: See Tom Wolfe, "The 'Me' Decade and the Third Great Awakening," *New York*, August 23, 1976.

36   **"Men and women marry"**: Peter Berger, *Invitation to Sociology: A Humanistic Perspective* (New York: Anchor, 1963), 35–36.

40   **Conscientious objection**: See *Welsh v. United States*, 398 U.S. 333 (1970) and *United States v. Seeger*, 380 U.S. 163 (1965).

46   **Historian**: Joshua B. Freeman, *American Empire: 1945–2000* (New York: Viking, 2012), 290.

69   **George Steiner**: *Errata: An Examined Life* (New Haven: Yale University Press, 1997), 49.

73   **"The Weak and the Strong"**: See Judith Shklar, "Jean-Jacques Rousseau and Equality," *Daedalus* 107 (3), and "The Liberalism of Fear," in *Liberalism and the Moral Life*, ed. Nancy L. Rosenblum (Cambridge: Harvard University Press, 1989), 21–38.

80   **Stephen Holmes**: *Passion and Constraint: On the Theory of Liberal Democracy* (Chicago: University of Chicago Press, 1995), 24. On method versus substance in political science, see also Ian Shapiro, *The Flight from Reality in the Human Sciences* (Princeton: Princeton University Press, 2007), 54 and *passim*.

85   **bell hooks**: *Teaching to Transgress: Education as the Practice of Freedom* (New York: Routledge, 1994), 3.

85   **Jay Parini**: *The Art of Teaching* (New York: Oxford University Press, 2005), 20.

85   **Instinctive preference**: Steiner, *Errata: An Examined Life*, 12.

104   **"Untested promise"**: Vivian Gornick, *The Situation and the Story* (New York: Farrar, Straus and Giroux, 2001), 58.

110   **Dale Peck**: *Visions and Revisions* (New York: Soho Press, 2015), 6.

111   **Gail Caldwell**: *New Life, New Instructions* (New York: Random House, 2014), 40.

125   **Later scholar**: Ira L. Stauber, *Neglected Policies: Constitutional Law and Legal Commentary* (Durham: University of North Carolina Press, 2002), 58.

127   **Federal funding**: See Roderick A. Ferguson, *The Reorder of Things* (Minneapolis: University of Minnesota Press, 2012), 49, and Christopher Newfield, *Unmaking the Public University* (Cambridge: Harvard University Press, 2008), 242.

127   **"From zero to sixty"**: Newfield, *Unmaking the Public University*, 242.

128   **University of California history**: *A Brief History of the University of California* (Berkeley: University of California Press, 2004), 60. See also Steiner, *Errata: An Examined Life*, 6.

128   **Rearticulation**: Andrew Delbanco, *College: What it Was, Is, and Should Be* (Princeton: Princeton University Press, 2012), 95.

See also David Damrosch, *We Scholars: Changing the Culture of the University* (Cambridge: Harvard University Press, 1995).

133 **Market values**: See Henry Giroux, *Neoliberalism's War on Higher Education* (Chicago: Haymarket Press, 2014), and Wendy Brown, *Undoing the Demos: Neoliberalism's Stealth Revolution* (Brooklyn: Zone Books, 2015), ch. VI.

133 **Tony Judt**: Tony Judt and Timothy Synder, *Thinking the Twentieth Century* (New York: Penguin, 2012), 361.

143 **"Potential saboteur"**: Martin Duberman, *Waiting to Land* (New York: New Press, 2009), 8.

143 **Hannah Arendt**: *Rahel Varnhagen: The Life of a Jewess* (1958), quoted in Kathleen B. Jones, *Diving for Pearls* (San Diego: Thinking Women's Books, 2013), Ch. 2.

165 **P. F. Kluge**: *Alma Mater* (Reading, MA: Addison Wesley, 1993).

165 **Joyce Carol Oates**: "A Widow's Story," *The New Yorker*, December 13, 2010.

167 **Mary Cantwell**: Memoir excerpt quoted in Paula Balzer, *Writing and Selling Your Memoir* (Cincinnati: Writer's Digest Books, 2011), 56.

169 **Worn out faculty**: For somewhat similar comments, see Jill Ker Conway's account of her tenure as president of Smith College in *A Woman's Education* (New York: Vintage, 2002).

186 **Esther Newton**: *Margaret Mead Made Me Gay: Personal Essays and Public Ideas* (Durham: Duke University Press, 2000), 224, 219.

187 **Queer Studies**: Eds. Robert J. Corber and Stephen Valocchi (Oxford: Blackwell, 2003).

189 **Toni McNaron**: *I Dwell in Possibility: A Memoir* (New York: Feminist Press at the City University of New York, 2001), 200.

189   "I am someone": *I Dwell in Possibility*, 205. See also Toni
       McNaron, *Poisoned Ivy: Lesbian and Gay Academics Confronting
       Homophobia* (Philadelphia: Temple University Press, 1997), 199.

194   Julian Barnes: *Nothing To Be Frightened Of* (New York: Vin-
       tage, 2009), 63.

197   Curriculum: Christopher J. Lucas, *Crisis in the Academy* (New
       York: Palgrave Macmillan, 1998), 161.

Acknowledgments

I am grateful to two wonderful freelance editors, Joy Johannessen and Priscilla Long, and to my literary agent, Cecelia Cancellaro, for their good counsel. It is also a pleasure to thank these friends and colleagues for comments on the manuscript at various stages: Lynn Powell, Molly Shanley, Sandy Zagarell, Alan Houston, Nancy Rosenblum, Kathy Jones, Tom Van Nortwick, John Hobbs, Ana Cara, Harlan Wilson, Diana Kahn, Judith Halberstam, Ian Abramson, Marian Yee, Wendy Brown, Keith Bybee, Clay Steinman, Jane Rhodes, Duchess Harris, Bogdan Popa, and Sarah Schulman, who also suggested the title.

I also would like to thank to thank Danielle McClellan for her copy-editing, Alan Childress at Quid Pro Books for his enthusiasm for the project, and Oberlin College for financial support.

I found direction from reading two books about memoir and I would like to thank the authors: Vivian Gornick, *The Situation and the Story* (New York: Farrar, Straus and Giroux, 2002) and Adair Lara, *Naked, Drunk, and Writing* (Berkeley: Ten Speed Press, 2010).

An earlier, shorter version of Chapter 9 was published in *The Queer Community: Continuing the Struggle for Social Justice* (San Diego: Birkdale, 2009), edited by Richard Greggory Johnson III.

Finally, I am grateful to UPS Store #4109 in Oberlin for copying and collating the many drafts of the manuscript.

H.N.H.
January 2016